SPECTRUM

NEW YORK
Test Prep

Grade 6

Align to Achieve
The Academic Standards e-Library

SPECTRUM

Frank Schaffer Publications®

Spectrum is an imprint of Frank Schaffer Publications.

Printed in the United States of America. All rights reserved. Except as permitted under the United States Copyright Act, no part of this publication may be reproduced or distributed in any form or by any means, or stored in a database or retrieval system, without prior written permission from the publisher, unless otherwise indicated. Frank Schaffer Publications is an imprint of School Specialty Children's Publishing. Copyright © 2005 School Specialty Children's Publishing.

Send all inquiries to:
Frank Schaffer Publications
3195 Wilson Drive NW
Grand Rapids, Michigan 49544

ISBN 0-7696-3496-6

1 2 3 4 5 6 7 8 9 10 PHXBK 09 08 07 06 05 04

Table of Contents

What's Inside?................ 5

Language Arts

Reading
Standards and What They Mean 7
  Practice Pages
  Identifying Genre 8
  Understanding Informational Texts 9
  Showing Understanding of
    Reading Through Writing 11
  Skimming Text 13
  Identifying Point of View 14
  Reading a Series of Steps 16
  Recording the Year's Reading 18
Mini-Test 1 19

Grammar and Usage of the English Language
Standards and What They Mean 20
  Practice Pages
  Subject and Verb Agreement 21
  Finding Main Ideas and Supporting Details .. 22
  Commas and Quotation Marks 24
  Commas and Semicolons 25
  Colons 26
  More Punctuation 27
  Verb Tenses 29

  Spelling Skills 30
  Spelling Correctly 32
  Revising 33
  Revising by Rearranging 34
  Revising by Adding or Deleting 36
  Using Reference Books 38
Mini-Test 2 39

Literature
Standards and What They Mean 41
  Practice Pages
  Comparing Books 42
  Similes and Metaphors 43
  Personification 45
  Analyzing Characters 46
  Analyzing Setting 48
  Setting and Plot 50
  Using Rhyme 51
  Examining Character Development 52
  Drawing Conclusions 54
  Making Predictions 55
Mini-Test 3 56

How Am I Doing? 58

Final Language Arts Test 59
  Answer Sheet 63

Mathematics

Arithmetic and Number Concepts
Standards and What They Mean............... 65
- Practice Pages
  - Place Value........................... 66
  - Expanded Notation..................... 67
  - Exponential and Scientific Notation....... 68
  - Rounding Numbers...................... 69
  - Rounding Decimals and Fractions........... 70
  - Using Estimation to Check Answers........ 71
  - Prime and Composite Numbers............. 72
  - Square Numbers........................ 73
  - Least Common Multiples and Greatest Common Divisors....................... 74
  - Whole Numbers (All Operations).......... 75
  - Adding and Subtracting Fractions......... 76
  - Multiplying Fractions and Mixed Numbers... 77
  - Dividing Fractions..................... 78
  - Percents, Decimals, and Fractions......... 79
  - Fractions to Decimals.................. 80
  - Decimal Operations..................... 81
  - Finding the Percent of a Number.......... 82
  - Using a Number Line.................... 83
  - Managing a Checking Account............ 84
  - Adding and Subtracting Integers on a Number Line........................ 85
  - Adding and Subtracting Negative Fractions on a Number Line..................... 86
  - Order of Operations.................... 87
  - Ratios................................ 88
  - Proportions........................... 89
  - Using Ratios and Proportions............. 90
- Mini-Test 1............................. 91

Geometry and Measurement Concepts
Standards and What They Mean............... 93
- Practice Pages
  - Measuring With a Ruler................. 94
  - Capacity Measurements—Metric........... 95
  - Mass Measurements—Metric.............. 96
  - Relating Metric Units to Customary Units.... 97
  - Time Measurement..................... 98
  - Area and Perimeter of Polygons.......... 99
  - Area of Irregular Shapes................ 100
  - Circumference and Area of Circles........ 101
  - Line and Point Graphs.................. 102
  - Identifying Angles..................... 103
  - Classifying Triangles................... 104
  - Comparing Plane Figures With Solid Figures........................ 105
  - Classifying Polygons................... 106
  - Classifying Quadrilaterals.............. 107
  - Classifying Polyhedrons................ 108
  - Cylinders, Cones, and Spheres........... 109
  - Similar and Congruent Figures........... 110
  - Parallel and Perpendicular Lines......... 111
  - Volume of Rectangular Prisms........... 112
  - Scale Drawings........................ 113
- Mini-Test 2............................ 114

Function and Algebra Concepts
Standards and What They Mean............... 116
- Practice Pages
  - Number Sequence...................... 117
  - Using Fractions to Show Ratios........... 118
  - Understanding Ratio and Proportion....... 119
  - Reading Ordered Number Pairs........... 120
  - Graphing Ordered Number Pairs.......... 121
  - Using Ordered Pairs to Construct Figures... 122
  - Understanding Functions................ 123
  - Applying the Order of Operations........ 124
  - Equivalent Open Sentences.............. 125
  - Using Variables and Equal Symbols....... 126
  - Identifying True Number Sentences....... 127
  - Writing True Number Sentences.......... 128
  - Using Variables....................... 129
  - Solving Equations..................... 130
- Mini-Test 3............................ 131

Statistics and Probability Concepts
Standards and What They Mean............... 132
- Practice Pages
  - Analyzing Data........................ 133
  - Using Bar Graphs...................... 134
  - Using Circle Graphs.................... 135
  - Using Stem and Leaf Plots............... 136
  - Comparing Line and Bar Graphs.......... 137
  - Using Appropriate Graphs............... 138
  - Mean, Median, Mode, and Range......... 139
  - Independent and Dependent Events....... 140
  - Probability With Dice.................. 141
  - Expressing Probability................. 143
  - Understanding Permutations............. 144
  - Using the Counting Principle............ 145
  - Identifying Sample Spaces.............. 146
- Mini-Test 4............................ 147

Mathematical Process
Standards and What They Mean............... 148
- Practice Pages
  - Solving Word Problems................. 149
  - Identifying Necessary Information........ 150
  - Using Strategies to Solve Problems........ 152
  - Applying Math to Real-World Situations.... 153
- Mini-Test 5............................ 154

How Am I Doing?............................ 155

Final Mathematics Test..................... 157
- Answer Sheet......................... 163

ANSWER KEY.................. 164

New York State Standards........ 174

What's Inside?

This workbook is designed to help you and your sixth grader understand what he or she will be expected to know on the New York sixth grade state tests.

Practice Pages

The workbook is divided into a language arts and mathematics section. Each section has practice activities that have questions similar to those that will appear on the state tests. Students should use a pencil to fill in the correct answers and to complete any writing on these activities.

New York City Standards

Before each practice section is a list of the standards covered by that section. The shaded *What it means* sections will help to explain any information in the standards that might be unfamiliar.

New York Standards

This book is set up using the most up-to-date New York City standards, as they are more current and broken into individual grade level (unlike New York State standards). The New York State standards and how they compare to the New York City standards are outlined in the back of this book.

Mini-Tests and Final Tests

Practice activities are grouped by standard. When each group is completed the student can move on to a mini-test that covers the material presented on those practice activities. After an entire set of standards and accompanying activities are completed, the student should take the final test, which incorporate materials from all the practice activities in that section.

Final Test Answer Sheet

The final tests have a separate answer sheet that mimics the style of the answer sheet the students will use on the state tests. The answer sheet appears at the end of each final test.

How Am I Doing?

The *How Am I Doing?* pages are designed to help students identify areas where they are proficient and areas where they still need more practice. Students can keep track of each of their mini-test scores on these pages.

Answer Key

Answers to all the practice activities, mini-tests, and final tests are listed by page number and appear at the end of the book.

Frequently Asked Questions

What kinds of information does my child have to know to pass the test?

The New York State Board of Education provides a list of the knowledge and skills that students are expected to master at each grade level. The practice activities in this workbook provide students with practice in each of these areas.

Are there special strategies or tips that will help my child do well?

The workbook provides sample questions that have content similar to that on the state tests. Test-taking tips are offered throughout the book.

How do I know what areas my child needs help in?

A special *How Am I Doing?* section will help you and your sixth grader evaluate his or her progress. It will pinpoint areas where more work is needed as well as areas where your student excels.

New York Language Arts Content Standards

The language arts section in the New York City Standards measures knowledge in three different areas:

1. Reading
2. Grammar and Usage of the English Language
3. Literature

The language arts section of the New York State Standards measures knowledge of language in four areas:

1.0 Language for Information and Understanding
   - *1.1:* Listening and Reading
   - *1.2:* Speaking and Writing

2.0 Language for Literary Response and Expression
   - *2.1:* Listening and Reading
   - *2.2:* Speaking and Writing

3.0 Language for Critical Analysis and Evaluation
   - *3.1:* Listening and Reading
   - *3.2:* Speaking and Writing

4.0 Language for Social Interaction
   - *4.1:* Listening and Speaking
   - *4.2:* Reading and Writing

New York Language Arts Table of Contents

Reading
- Standards and What They Mean 7
- Practice Pages 8
- Mini-Test 1 19

Grammar and Usage of the English Language
- Standards and What They Mean. 20
- Practice Pages 21
- Mini-Test 2 39

Literature
- Standards and What They Mean. 41
- Practice Pages 42
- Mini-Test 3 56

How Am I Doing? 58

Final Language Arts Test 59
- Answer Sheet 63

Language Arts Standards

1.0 Reading
By the end of the school year, students should:
- **1.A** Read and understand:
  - **1.A.1** At least twenty-five books.
  - **1.A.2** At least four books about one subject, or by the same writer, or in one genre of literature. *(See page 8.)*

> **What it means:**
> - **Genre** is a type, or category, of literature. Some examples of genre include fiction, biographies, poetry, and fables. Each genre is characterized by various differences in form. For example, a fable differs from the broader category of fiction in that it has a moral or character lesson.

  - **1.A.3** Informational texts (such as reference materials, newspapers and magazines, and textbooks). *(See pages 9–10.)*
- **1.B** Show evidence of understanding their reading both in writing and classroom discussion. *(See pages 11–12.)*
- **1.C** Skim texts to get an overview of content or locate specific information. *(See page 13.)*
- **1.D** Put together ideas, information, and points of view from several books. *(See pages 14–15.)*
- **1.E** Read silently and independently.
- **1.F** Read a series of steps to accomplish a task (for example, follow a recipe). *(See pages 16–17.)*
- **1.G** Use technology to support and extend reading.
- **1.H** Keep a record of what has been read, reflecting goals and accomplishments. *(See page 18.)*

Name _____ Date _____

Language Arts
Reading

1.A.2

Identifying Genre

DIRECTIONS: Based on the passages below, identify the genre of literature of each.

 **Clue** — *Genre* is a type, or category, of literature. Some examples of genre include fiction, nonfiction, biographies, poetry, and fables.

1. **Act IV**
   Timothy enters his apartment and finds the furniture overturned and things thrown from the drawers. He picks up the telephone and dials 9-1-1.
   TIMOTHY: (fearfully) Yes, I need to report a break-in! (pause) No, I haven't searched the entire apartment. (pause) Do you really think they could still be here?!

   _____

2. The children awoke to a happy sight.
   While they were sleeping, the world had turned white.
   Their mother peered into their room and said, "No school today. Go back to bed!"

   _____

3. Raccoon sat on the beach eating his potato. Before each bite he dipped the potato into the water. Monkey watched him from his perch in the tree and wondered about this curious habit.

   _____

4. The Himalayas are sometimes called the tallest mountains on earth. The truth is that several underwater ranges are even higher.
   A passage like this would most likely be found in a book of _____ .
   - Ⓐ fables
   - Ⓑ facts
   - Ⓒ tall tales
   - Ⓓ adventure stories

DIRECTIONS: Based on the titles below, identify the genre of literature of each.

5. *King Arthur and the Blazing Sword*
   - Ⓕ novel
   - Ⓖ play
   - Ⓗ legend
   - Ⓙ folktale

6. *Adventure to Venus*
   - Ⓐ novel
   - Ⓑ play
   - Ⓒ legend
   - Ⓓ folktale

7. "*Ode to an Owl, the Wisest of Fowl*"
   - Ⓕ play
   - Ⓖ legend
   - Ⓗ novel
   - Ⓙ poetry

8. *How Zebra Got His Stripes*
   - Ⓐ legend
   - Ⓑ folktale
   - Ⓒ poetry
   - Ⓓ novel

9. *Abraham Lincoln: His Life Story*
   - Ⓕ legend
   - Ⓖ poem
   - Ⓗ novel
   - Ⓙ biography

Name _____ Date _____

Language Arts Reading

1.A.3

Understanding Informational Texts

DIRECTIONS: Read the following passage from a textbook. Then, answer the questions on the next page.

The Sequoia

One natural wonder of the world is among the oldest and largest living things on earth. It is the sequoia, a tree that once grew in plentiful varieties in forests over much of the world. Today, sequoias are found mainly in California. California is the only place where the two kinds of true sequoias—the redwood and the giant sequoia—still grow.

The redwood is the tallest living tree. It is found in the coastal mountains of northern California and southern Oregon. Growing in this warm, moist climate, the redwoods reach over 300 feet high. That's as tall as a 30-story building! The trunks of redwood trees are often more than 10 feet in diameter. The bark can be as thick as 12 inches. The redwood gets its name from the color of its wood, which turns from light to dark red as it weathers. Redwoods are sometimes called "California redwoods" or "coasts" since they grow along the Pacific coast of California.

The other true sequoia is the giant sequoia, which grows only on the western slopes of the Sierra Nevada Mountains in California. Once, the giant sequoias grew in many parts of the Northern Hemisphere. Today, they are found in only 70 groves. These giant sequoia groves are high in the mountains at elevations of 5,000 to 7,800 feet. Although giant sequoias do not grow as tall as redwoods, their trunks are much larger. Some trunks are as large as 100 feet around the base.

The largest tree in the world is found in Sequoia National Park. Named the General Sherman Tree, it stands 272.4 feet high and measures 101.6 feet around its base. Scientists believe that this single tree could produce over 600,000 board feet of lumber!

The giant sequoia is classified as an evergreen tree. It grows scale-like needles up to one-half inch long and produces woody oval-shaped cones about two to three inches long. Although lightning has destroyed the tops of many of the trees, they are considered to be among the hardiest of living things.

Scientists have dated many giant sequoias to be several thousand years old. The age is determined by counting the growth rings on a tree's trunk. Each growth ring stands for one year. Scientists have estimated that the General Sherman Tree is at least 3,500 years old, and so it becomes not only the world's largest tree, but also one of the oldest living things on earth.

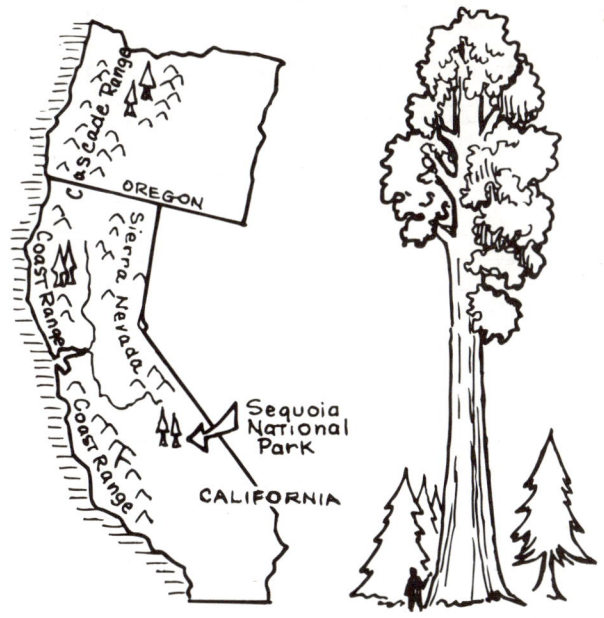

GO

Name _____ Date _____

DIRECTIONS: Fill in the blanks with information from the textbook passage on the previous page.

1. The giant sequoia once grew in many parts of the _____ Hemisphere.

2. Today, the giant sequoia is found in only _____ groves high in the mountains at elevations of _____ to _____ feet.

3. Sequoias are found mainly in _____ , where only _____ kinds still grow: _____ and _____ .

4. What resources would you use to check the accuracy of the information given in the passage?
   _____
   _____
   _____
   _____

5. **The author of this passage is most likely to support which of the following?**
   - Ⓐ producing 600,000 board feet of lumber from the General Sherman Tree
   - Ⓑ studying redwood trees instead of sequoias
   - Ⓒ encouraging people to visit Sequoia National Park
   - Ⓓ allowing lightning to burn down the tops of trees

6. **Summarize in two or three sentences the author's purpose in writing about sequoia trees in this passage.**
   _____
   _____
   _____
   _____
   _____
   _____
   _____
   _____
   _____
   _____

Language Arts

1.B

Showing Understanding of Reading Through Writing

Reading

DIRECTIONS: Read the passages comparing Antarctica and the Sahara. Then, answer the questions on the next page.

Antarctica

Antarctica is the continent surrounding the South Pole. It contains 90 percent of the world's ice. Antarctica is the coldest and most desolate region on earth. It covers 5,400,000 square miles. Much of the land is buried under snow and ice one mile thick. The winter temperatures reach −100°F in the interior of the continent. On the coast, the temperatures fall below −40°F.

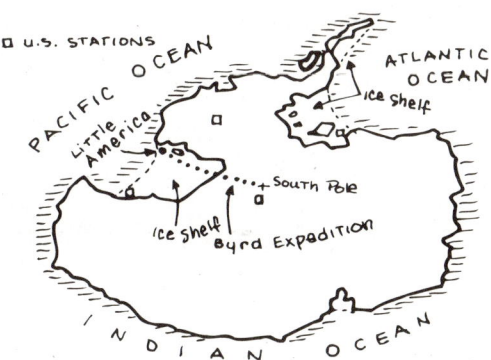

The interior of Antarctica is a frozen, lifeless region. The only animal life in Antarctica is found on the coastline or in the sea. Penguins, seals, whales, and other fish and birds live in or close to the coastal waters. These animals live on food from the sea.

The ancient Greeks called the North Pole the "Arctic." They believed that land at the South Pole must also exist. They called this supposed land "Antarctica," meaning the opposite of Arctic.

In 1928, Commander Richard E. Byrd of the U.S. Navy led a famous expedition to the South Pole. He and his men set up a base called Little America. Until his death in 1957, Byrd took five expeditions to Antarctica. He helped establish scientific research bases and led the largest Antarctic expedition in history with over 4,000 men and 13 ships.

The Sahara

Stretching almost 3,000 miles across North Africa, the Sahara Desert is an incredible natural wonder of sand, rock, and gravel. The Sahara covers over 3,500,000 square miles, which makes it by far the largest desert on earth. It extends west to east from the Atlantic Ocean to the Red Sea.

The name *Sahara* comes from an Arabic word, "Sahra," which means *desert*. Because of the unusually low rainfall, the sun-scorched land and blistering winds make the Sahara the hottest region in the world during the summer. A sandy surface may reach a temperature of 170°F. The cloudless skies allow the daytime air temperature to reach 100°F. At night, the temperature often drops 40 to 50 degrees.

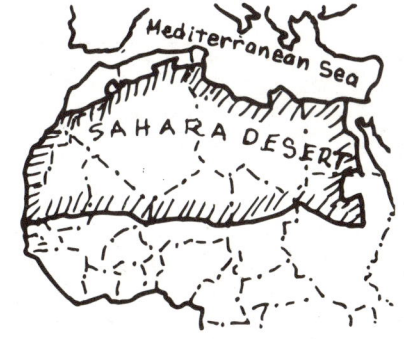

The Sahara's only vegetation is found near wells, springs, or streams. These fertile areas are called *oases*. Throughout the desert are many dry streambeds, called *wadis*. During a rare rain, they temporarily fill up with water. The Sahara supports some animal life, too—camels, lizards, and the addax, a desert antelope.

Some people of the Sahara live in tents, which allows them to move more easily in search of grassy areas. These people, called *nomads*, tend flocks of sheep, camels, or goats. Other people raise crops on land that has been irrigated.

GO

Name _____ Date _____

1. **What challenges are presented by both regions because of their climate?**

   _____
   _____
   _____
   _____
   _____
   _____
   _____
   _____
   _____
   _____

2. **How have humans and/or animals adapted to life in both regions?**

   _____
   _____
   _____
   _____
   _____
   _____
   _____
   _____
   _____
   _____

3. **If you had to choose to go on an expedition to either Antarctica or the Sahara, which place would you choose? Why?**

   _____
   _____
   _____
   _____
   _____
   _____
   _____
   _____
   _____
   _____
   _____
   _____
   _____
   _____
   _____
   _____
   _____
   _____
   _____
   _____
   _____
   _____

STOP

Name _____ Date _____

Language Arts

1.C

Skimming Texts

Reading

DIRECTIONS: Skim the passage, then read the questions. Refer back to the passage to find the answers. You don't have to read the story over again for each question.

The Ship of the Desert

Nomads who crisscross the Sahara Desert of North Africa rely on a most unique animal for transportation—the dromedary, or one-humped camel. Because it is indispensable to desert travel, the dromedary is sometimes called the *ship of the desert.*

Several factors make the dromedary suitable for long desert trips. It can go for long periods without nourishment. The hump on a camel's back serves as its food reserve. When it has little to eat, it converts the fat from its hump into energy. The camel's hump can weigh up to 80 pounds or more. When the animal has to rely on its reservoir of fat, the hump becomes much smaller. Thus, it is easy to recognize a well-fed camel by the size of its hump.

Many people believe that camels store water in their humps. This is not true. Their ability to go for days without drinking is due to other factors. First, camels are able to drink large quantities of water at one time. Some have been known to gulp 53 gallons in one day. Second, the camel sweats very little and can tolerate greater body temperatures. Consequently, it retains most of the water it drinks and can travel several hundred miles before replenishing its supply.

Other physical characteristics enable the camel to endure harsh desert conditions. It can completely close its nostrils, thus protecting it from the stinging effects of sandstorms. Its eyes are shielded from sand and sun by overhanging lids and long lashes, and its broad, padded feet keep it from sinking into the soft sand. No other animal is better equipped for life in the desert than the camel.

1. **Based on skimming the text, what is the passage about?**
   - Ⓐ the Sahara Desert
   - Ⓑ the dromedary camel
   - Ⓒ ships in North Africa
   - Ⓓ nomads

2. **What is the main idea of this passage?**
   - Ⓕ The dromedary is the ideal animal for desert life.
   - Ⓖ The camel's hump serves as its food reservoir.
   - Ⓗ The dromedary is called the *ship of the desert.*
   - Ⓙ Camels do not store water in their humps.

3. **Which characteristic does not help the camel to survive in the desert?**
   - Ⓐ A camel can drink up to 53 gallons of water in one day.
   - Ⓑ A camel can close its nostrils.
   - Ⓒ A camel sweats very little.
   - Ⓓ A camel is indispensable to desert travel.

4. **What cannot be concluded from reading this passage?**
   - Ⓕ A camel can survive a long time without eating.
   - Ⓖ A dromedary camel is easier to ride than a Bactrian camel.
   - Ⓗ Camels have many features that equip them for cold weather.
   - Ⓙ Both G and H

13

Name _____ Date _____

Language Arts Reading

1.D # Identifying Points of View

DIRECTIONS: Read the passage. Then, answer the questions on the next page.

The World Series

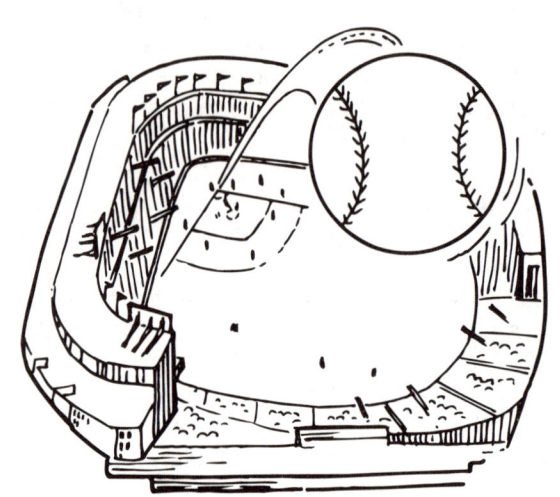

Baseball is an important part of American culture and history. The World Series is the most exciting and important sporting event of the year because it names the national champion in America's favorite pastime.

In spite of what the title says, the World Series is actually not a championship open to the world. The World Series matches the American League champion team against the National League champion team. The first team to win four games out of seven wins the World Series.

The World Series was first played in 1903. The American League champions, the Boston Pilgrims, played the National League champions, the Pittsburgh Pirates. The Boston Pilgrims, now named the Boston Red Sox, won this first World Series.

Although the World Series seemed to be off to a great start in 1903, the next year was a different story. In 1904, the New York Giants refused to play the Boston Pilgrims in the World Series. To this day, no one is sure why they refused, but 1904 was the only year in World Series history that did not have a world championship series.

For a team to make it to the World Series takes months of hard work and a lot of talent. Most teams play more than 150 games between April and October of each year. Many great baseball players, such as Babe Ruth, Jackie Robinson, Joe Di Maggio, and Lou Gehrig, have played in the World Series.

Many World Series records have been broken over the years. But in 1956, a little-known player named Don Larsen pitched a no-hitter game for the New York Yankees. His record has never been broken.

The New York Yankees have won more World Series championships than any other team in history. No matter who wins the title, the World Series remains one of the most popular events each year for sport fans. In fact, there is even a World Series for the youngest players. Unlike the adult World Series, the Little League World Series includes teams from other countries. Taiwan has won more than any other foreign country.

 GO

14

Name _____   Date _____

1. Which of the following statements best represents the author's purpose in writing about the World Series?

   - Ⓐ The teams that play in the World Series should both be from the National League.
   - Ⓑ The New York Giants did not have a good reason for refusing to play in 1904.
   - Ⓒ Teams that get to the World Series have worked hard for months.
   - Ⓓ A World Series is not complete without a good snack to eat.

2. If the headline "World Series Deemed Unnecessary" appeared in a local paper, how might the author of the passage on the previous page respond?

   _____
   _____
   _____
   _____

3. If you were looking at the following titles in a local bookstore, which would you guess was written by the author of this piece?

   - Ⓕ *Baseball Foul-Ups Through the Ages*
   - Ⓖ *A Comprehensive History of Sports*
   - Ⓗ *The Most Exciting Games of the World Series*
   - Ⓙ *Reasons to Abolish Baseball Leagues*

4. What phrases or sentences in the passage describe the author's point of view about the World Series?

   _____
   _____
   _____
   _____
   _____

5. What is your opinion, or point of view, about the World Series? Do you think it is the most exciting and important sporting event of the year? Write a few sentences in which you describe your point of view.

   _____
   _____
   _____
   _____
   _____
   _____
   _____
   _____
   _____
   _____

STOP

Reading a Series of Steps

DIRECTIONS: Read the passage. Then, answer the questions on the next page.

Preparing a Budget

Always running out of money? Have no idea where your money goes? Saving for a special trip, activity, or object? If you answered *yes* to any of these questions, it is time to plan a budget and stick to it.

Budgets have a bad rap as being too restrictive or too hard to follow. In reality, a budget can be very simple, and understanding how to use one can help you save for special things. There are three easy steps to follow.

The first step in building a livable budget is to record your spending habits. Look at your expenditures. Do you buy your lunch? Do you buy a soft drink or even water from a machine? You may discover you spend money foolishly. Buying a candy bar for $0.50 every day may seem insignificant, but by the end of the month, it adds up to $15.00. Instead, put a snack in your backpack.

The next step is determining your debits and credits. Look at what money comes in and what goes out. If you have determined your spending habits, you know what your debits are. Credits might be harder to determine if you do not have a job. Determine all the ways you get money. For example, count the dollars you earn or money given to you as presents. How much each week do you have available to spend? What are your sources of income?

If you do not have a regular source of income, you need to find ways to make money. Do you have an allowance? Can you negotiate with your parents to raise your allowance? Offer to do more chores or special jobs that will increase your income. Check out the neighborhood. Lawn work and baby-sitting are two jobs that you might like. Remember, your debits should not be more than your credits.

The last step is determining your cash flow and savings goals. How much money do you have available each week to spend? You might budget a small cash flow for yourself because you want to save for a new pair of skis, which means you might earn $10.00 a week, but only allow yourself to spend $3.00. Look at three important categories. How much money do you wish to save? How much money do you need for essentials? How much money do you want for frivolous activities? Determining the balance between savings goals and cash flow is an important decision for any budget.

GO

Name _____ Date _____

1. Define the following terms. Then, write the sentence or phrase that helped you determine its definition.

   expenditures _____

   _____

   debit _____

   _____

   credit _____

   _____

   cash flow _____

   _____

2. **List the three steps in preparing a budget.**

   Step 1 _____

   Step 2 _____

   Step 3 _____

3. **Describe your current approach to a budget. Use all the vocabulary from question 1 in your response.**

   _____

   _____

   _____

4. **After looking at your current approach to a budget, make yourself a revised budget using the chart below. Be sure that your debits do not exceed your credits!**

Date	Credits	Debits
Total		

Name _____ Date _____

Language Arts   **Reading**

1.H   # Recording the Year's Reading

DIRECTIONS: Pick at least two reading goals for the year. For example, you might want to read all of the books in a particular series, or you may wish to learn one new word every week.

The grid below will help you keep a record of all of the reading you've done over the year. Remember to fill it in regularly to show what you've read. Place a star beside the titles of the books that helped you reach your goals.

Reading Goal #1: _____

_____

Reading Goal #2: _____

_____

	Title	Author	Date Completed	Genre (biography, science fiction, western, etc.)
1.				
2.				
3.				
4.				
5.				
6.				
7.				
8.				
9.				
10.				
11.				
12.				
13.				
14.				
15.				
16.				
17.				
18.				
19.				
20.				
21.				
22.				
23.				
24.				
25.				

Name _____ Date _____

Language Arts

1.0

For pages 8–17

Reading

Mini-Test 1

DIRECTIONS: Read the following passage and answer the questions.

Daedalus

According to a Greek myth, Daedalus was an inventor who had a son named Icarus. Daedalus designed the labyrinth, a maze of complicated passages that is very difficult to escape. Minos, the king of the island Crete, used the labyrinth to hide a monster called *Minotaur,* who was half man and half bull.

Daedalus did something to anger Minos, and the king made Daedalus and Icarus prisoners in the labyrinth. One day, Daedalus got an idea as he was watching birds fly. He asked Icarus to gather up all the bird feathers he could find. Then, using the feathers and some wax, Daedalus created two large pairs of wings. Soon he and Icarus were on their way over the walls of the labyrinth.

DIRECTIONS: Read the following events and answer question 1.

Q. Minos hid the Minotaur in the labyrinth.

R. Daedalus made Minos angry.

S. _____

T. Daedalus watched birds flying.

U. Daedalus and Icarus escaped.

1. Which event is missing between R and T?
    - (A) Icarus melted wax.
    - (B) Daedalus went to Crete.
    - (C) Icarus collected feathers.
    - (D) Daedalus and Icarus were imprisoned.

2. Which of the following best describes Icarus?
    - (F) a Greek prince
    - (G) a supernatural creature
    - (H) an inventor
    - (J) an innocent captive

3. Which of the following was most likely the source of Daedalus's ideas for inventions?
    - (A) Greek architecture
    - (B) the world of nature
    - (C) books and drawings
    - (D) the suggestions of King Minos

4. This passage is which genre of literature?
    - (F) biography
    - (G) fiction
    - (H) nonfiction
    - (J) poetry

STOP

19

Language Arts Standards

2.0 Grammar and Usage of the English Language

By the end of the school year, students should demonstrate correct use of:

- **2.A** Grammar, including correct subject/verb agreement. *(See page 21.)*
- **2.B** Paragraph structure, including main and supporting ideas. *(See pages 22–23.)*
- **2.C** Punctuation, including semicolons, quotation marks, commas, and colons. *(See pages 24–28.)*
- **2.D** Sentence construction, including correct subject/verb agreement and verb tense. *(See page 29.)*
- **2.E** Spelling strategies for sixth-grade content-area vocabulary. *(See pages 30–32.)*

By the end of the school year, students should be able to revise work by:

- **2.F** Making their writing easier to understand. *(See page 33.)*
- **2.G** Rearranging the sequence of words, sentences, and paragraphs. *(See pages 34–35.)*
- **2.H** Adding or deleting details and explanations. *(See pages 36–37.)*
- **2.I** Using dictionaries, reference books, and sample papers to assist in editing. *(See page 38.)*
- **2.J** Learning word processing skills.

Name _____ Date _____

Language Arts

2.A

Subject and Verb Agreement

Grammar and Usage of the English Language

Examples:

- A singular subject must have a singular verb as a partner. A plural subject must have a plural verb as a partner. Example: *People are living longer in many countries. People* is a plural subject, so the plural verb *are* is used with it.
- If two singular words appear together as compound subjects, the verb will be plural. Example: *Hank and Sandy think they passed the test*, not *Hank and Sandy thinks they passed the test*.
- If a compound subject is joined with *either—or, neither—nor*, the verb must agree with the subject that is closer to the verb. Example: *Neither my brother nor I think we look alike. Either my dog or my cats are making noise outside.*
- Words such as *everyone, anyone, no one, somebody, someone, something* are called singular indefinite pronouns. They always require a singular verb. Example: *Everyone who comes to my party is bringing a gift*, not *Everyone who comes to my party are bringing a gift*.

DIRECTIONS: Write the correct verb form to match each subject in the story below.

Cormorants _____ (is, are) birds that help people. In some countries, this type of bird _____ (is, are) used to help catch fish! Great fishermen (or fisherbirds), cormorants _____ (fly, flies) around fishing grounds. Fishermen watching them know where the fish _____ (is, are). Some fishermen _____ (catch, catches) cormorants. They _____ (tie, ties) long cords to the birds, then _____ (take, takes) them out on their boats. When the birds _____ (dive, dives) under the water to catch fish, the fishermen _____ (keep, keeps) them from making off with the fish. Cormorants _____ (is, are) related to pelicans. Most cormorants _____ (perch, perches) in trees, on rocks, and on the edges of cliffs. They _____ (has, have) webbed feet.

DIRECTIONS: Circle the correct verb in each sentence.

1. Those toys (is, are) loved by most children.

2. There (is, are) two kids who missed the bus.

3. Neither my cat nor my dogs (like, likes) to eat pet food.

4. There (is, are) no reasons for you to miss school today.

5. Facts (is, are) facts, and you can't deny them.

6. Many movie monsters (is, are) truly scary.

7. Either you or your sister (is, are) going to clean that room.

8. Five tomatoes (is, are) growing on the vine.

STOP

Finding Main Ideas and Supporting Details

DIRECTIONS: Read the passage and answer the questions on the next page.

Yellowstone

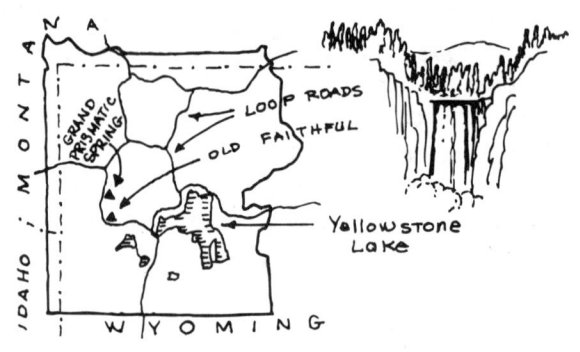

Yellowstone National Park is the site of some of the most famous natural wonders in the world, including geysers, hot springs, deep canyons, waterfalls, and great evergreen forests. Yellowstone is the oldest national park in the United States. It covers an area of land approximately 60 by 50 miles. Most of the land is located in the state of Wyoming, but it also spreads into Idaho and Montana. Scientists believe that the landscape of Yellowstone was created by a series of volcanic eruptions thousands of years ago. Molten rock, called *magma*, remains under the park. The heat from the magma produces the 200 geysers and thousands of hot springs for which Yellowstone is well-known.

Of all the wonders in Yellowstone, the main attraction is a famous geyser, Old Faithful. Approximately every 65 minutes, Old Faithful erupts for three to five minutes. The geyser erupts in a burst of boiling water that jumps 100 feet into the air. Other geysers in the park produce a spectacular sight, but none are as popular as Old Faithful.

Geysers may differ in frequency of eruption and size, but they all work in much the same way. As water seeps into the ground, it collects around the hot magma. The heated water produces steam, which rises and pushes up the cooler water above it. When the pressure becomes too great, the water erupts into the air. The cooled water falls back to the ground, and the cycle begins again.

The magma under the park also produces bubbling hot springs and mud pools, called *mudpots*. The largest hot spring in Yellowstone is Grand Prismatic Spring. It measures 370 feet wide.

Yellowstone Lake measures over 20 miles long and 14 miles wide. It is the largest high-altitude lake in North America. It lies almost 8,000 feet above sea level.

Evergreen forests of pine, fir, and spruce trees cover 90 percent of Yellowstone Park. Two hundred species of birds are found in Yellowstone. More than 40 kinds of other animals live in Yellowstone, which is the largest wildlife preserve in the United States. Visitors to the park may see bears, bison, cougars, moose, and mule deer.

Yellowstone National Park offers more than 1,000 miles of hiking trails. Over 2 million people visit the park each year.

Name _____   Date _____

DIRECTIONS: Circle the correct answer.

1. **Choose the title that best reflects the main idea of this passage.**
   - (A) *Yellowstone's High-Altitude Lake*
   - (B) *An Amazing Wildlife Preserve*
   - (C) *Old Faithful Still Faithful*
   - (D) *The Natural Wonders of Yellowstone*

2. **What is the main idea of the second paragraph?**
   - (F) Yellowstone Lake is the largest high-altitude lake in North America.
   - (G) The main attraction in Yellowstone is the geyser named Old Faithful.
   - (H) Ninety percent of Yellowstone is covered by evergreen forests.
   - (J) Yellowstone is home to some of the world's most famous natural wonders.

3. **What is the main idea of the third paragraph?**
   - (A) None of the geysers are as popular as Old Faithful.
   - (B) Heated steam pushes up cooler water, which eventually erupts.
   - (C) Geysers all work in much the same way.
   - (D) Yellowstone is the largest wildlife preserve in the United States.

DIRECTIONS: Fill in the web below based on information in the passage. Include two supporting details for each natural wonder.

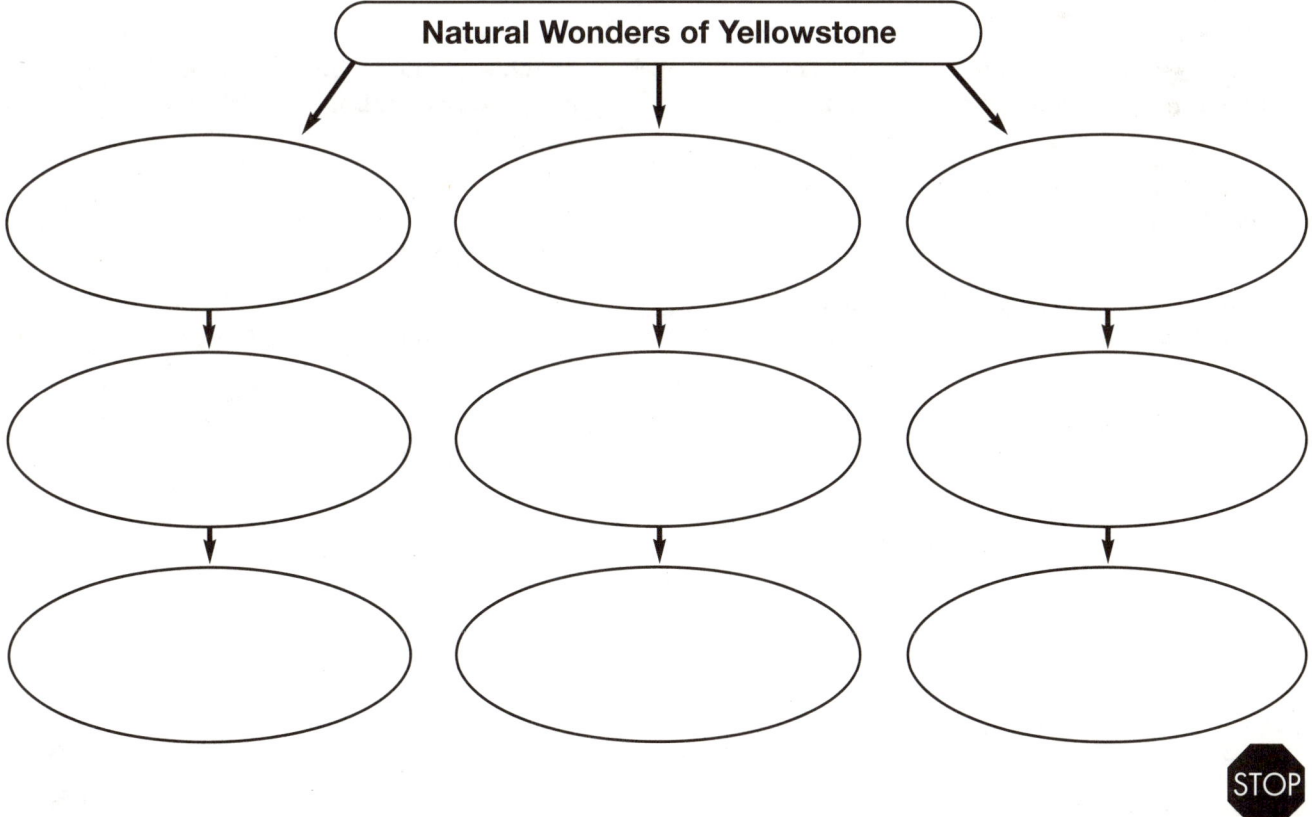

STOP

23

Commas and Quotation Marks

Language Arts 2.C

Grammar and Usage of the English Language

DIRECTIONS: Insert the correct punctuation and capitalization in the quotations below.

> **Examples:**
> - When a conversation is written out, quotation marks are used around the speaker's exact words. A comma is used before the quotations when the quoted speaker's name comes first. Example: *Mark Twain said, "Always do right. This will gratify some people, and astonish the rest."*
> - When the quoted speaker's name comes last, a comma, question mark, or exclamation point is used to end the quotation. A period is used after the quoted speaker's name. Example: *"There is only one success—to be able to spend your life in your own way," said Christopher Morley.*
> - When a quotation is interrupted by the quoted speaker's name, commas are used to separate the name from the quotation. Example: *"Life is a garment we continue to alter," said David McCord, "but which never seems to fit."*
> - When there are two sentences in a quotation, the name of the person speaking is followed by a period. Example: *"Maud went to college. Sadie stayed at home," said Gwendolyn Brooks. "Sadie scraped life with a fine-tooth comb."*

1. Mark Twain said work consists of whatever a body is obliged to do. . . . Play consists of whatever a body is not obliged to do

2. April prepares her green traffic light and the world thinks Go said Christopher Morley

3. That's one small step for a man said Neil Armstrong and one giant leap for mankind

4. Injustice anywhere is a threat to justice everywhere said Martin Luther King, Jr.

5. Training is everything said Mark Twain the peach was once a bitter almond; cauliflower is nothing but cabbage with a college education

6. Anne Frank said whoever is happy will make others happy too

7. Strength through joy said Robert Ley

8. Abraham Lincoln said stand with anybody that stands right. Stand with him while he is right and part with him when he goes wrong

Name _____ Date _____

Language Arts
2.C

Commas and Semicolons

Grammar and Usage of the English Language

 Remember that commas separate clauses. Semicolons can replace conjunctions and connect two related independent clauses.

DIRECTIONS: Correctly place commas or semicolons in the sentences below.

1. Marcy and I bolted from the car and we raced to the duck pond.

2. At first, Marcy was ahead I was behind by only a second.

3. Then, Marcy speeded up and I got out of breath.

4. Soon, Marcy passed me I didn't have a chance.

5. Marcy was really flying but she didn't look where she was going.

6. The duck pond was right in front of Marcy but she couldn't stop.

7. Marcy had to stop or she would land right in the duck pond.

8. Suddenly, there was a splash all the ducks were squawking.

9. A large, featherless object had just landed in their little world and they were not happy.

10. Marcy had made a big splash but she had won the race.

DIRECTIONS: Write each of the following using the correct punctuation and capitalization.

11. Closing:
    sincerely
    _____

12. Greeting of a business letter:
    dear sir
    _____

13. Write a greeting to a friend.
    _____

14. Greeting of a business letter:
    dear ms. sorenson
    _____

15. Greeting of a friendly letter:
    dear Julie
    _____

16. Write a greeting to your mom.
    _____

Name _____ Date _____

Language Arts
2.C

Colons

Grammar and Usage of the English Language

> **Examples:**
> - A **colon** is used before two or more items introduced by words such as *the following, as follows,* or *these,* or by a specific number. Examples: *For the hike, you will need the following: sturdy shoes, a backpack, and socks. There are four basic directions: north, south, east, and west.*
> - A colon is not used before direct objects, predicate nouns, or objects of prepositions. Examples: *For the hike, you will need sturdy shoes, a backpack, and socks.* (direct objects) *Supplies needed for the hike are sturdy shoes, a backpack, and socks.* (predicate nouns) *She walked to the north, to the south, to the east, and to the west.* (objects of preposition)

DIRECTIONS: Rewrite the sentences below correctly.

1. At the grocery store, we need to buy the following chicken, lettuce, and salad dressing.

   _____
   _____
   _____

2. Matthew likes pepperoni, onion, and green pepper: on his pizza.

   _____
   _____
   _____

3. There are five people: in our family Mom, Dad, Jarad, Scott, and me.

   _____
   _____
   _____

4. We need people to play these: parts the detective, the detective's assistant, and the old man.

   _____
   _____
   _____

DIRECTIONS: Insert colons where necessary and delete colons that are not necessary. Write *C* after each sentence below that is correct.

5. On your trip, remember to pack toothpaste, a toothbrush, and extra socks. _____

6. Sandie's favorite subjects are math, spelling, science, and art. _____

7. Tiffany likes these games soccer, baseball, and volleyball. _____

8. Jack put the following on his sandwich: ham, cheese, mustard, mayonnaise, and pickles. _____

9. I want to visit these: countries Mexico, Spain, and France. _____

26

Name _____ Date _____

Language Arts

2.C

More Punctuation

Grammar and Usage of the English Language

Examples:

A. Did you remember to brush your teeth
- (A) .
- (B) ?
- (C) !
- (D) None

Answer: B

B. "Keep up the good work," said Mrs. Goodwin.
- (F) ,
- (G) "
- (H) .
- (J) None

Answer: J

DIRECTIONS: Correctly place missing punctuation marks at the end of or within the sentences below. If there are no mistakes, choose "None."

Clue

Look carefully at all the answer choices before you choose the one you think is correct. The missing punctuation mark may be at the end of the sentence or within it. Remember to look in both places.

---

1. The yellow daffodils are very pretty
   - (A) ,
   - (B) .
   - (C) ?
   - (D) None

2. The robin, our state bird, lays blue eggs.
   - (F) ;
   - (G) !
   - (H) .
   - (J) None

3. "Stop, she called.
   - (A) "
   - (B) .
   - (C) "
   - (D) None

4. We visited Michigan Ohio, and Illinois.
   - (F) .
   - (G) ,
   - (H) ;
   - (J) None

5. "Hurry! School starts in ten minutes" said Isabel.
   - (A) .
   - (B) ?
   - (C) ,
   - (D) None

6. My favorite book A Wrinkle in Time, was already checked out.
   - (F) .
   - (G) :
   - (H) ,
   - (J) None

27

Name _____ Date _____

DIRECTIONS: Fill in the circle for the choice that has a punctuation error. If there are no mistakes, choose "No mistakes."

7. Ⓐ Our teacher Ms. Matthews, is
    Ⓑ treating the class to ice cream sundaes
    Ⓒ at Dairy Delight, my favorite ice cream shop.
    Ⓓ No mistakes.

8. Ⓕ Do you think you will complete
    Ⓖ your report by Saturday.
    Ⓗ I want to go to the beach on Sunday afternoon.
    Ⓙ No mistakes.

9. Ⓐ "I miss Grandpa," said Casey,
    Ⓑ "Can we see him again soon?"
    Ⓒ She loved her grandpa very much.
    Ⓓ No mistakes.

10. Ⓕ 8789 Rachel Dr.
    Ⓖ Aarontown, MI 49543
    Ⓗ May 22 2002.
    Ⓙ No mistakes.

11. Ⓐ Dear Melvin
    Ⓑ   I was so pleased to hear you won the
    Ⓒ scholarship to computer camp. Good job!
    Ⓓ No mistakes.

12. Ⓕ You will have to show me all you learned?
    Ⓖ Sincerely,
    Ⓗ Margie
    Ⓙ No mistakes.

DIRECTIONS: Choose the word or words that fit best in the blank and show the correct punctuation.

13. _____ please remember to wash your hands.
    Ⓐ Brewster
    Ⓑ Brewster:
    Ⓒ Brewster,
    Ⓓ "Brewster"

14. The _____ bite was bigger than its bark.
    Ⓕ dogs
    Ⓖ dog's
    Ⓗ dogs's
    Ⓙ dogs'

15. Charlene needed to bring _____ to the picnic.
    Ⓐ plates, napkins, and cups
    Ⓑ plates napkins and cups
    Ⓒ plates, napkins, and cups,
    Ⓓ plates, napkins and, cups

16. This bus is _____ we'll have to catch the next one.
    Ⓕ full
    Ⓖ full,
    Ⓗ full;
    Ⓙ full:

Name _____ Date _____

Language Arts
2.D

Verb Tenses

Grammar and Usage of the English Language

> **Examples:**
>
> **Verbs** name an action in a sentence and also tell when the action happens. The **tense** of the verb tells when the action happens.
>
> - The **present tense** of a verb indicates that an action is happening now. Example: *Rabbits are popular pets.*
> - The **past tense** of a verb indicates that an action has already happened. Example: *Rabbits were not popular in the past.*
> - The **future tense** of a verb names an action that will take place in the future. The helping verb *will* is used to form the future tense. Example: *Rabbits will remain popular in the future.*

DIRECTIONS: Write *past, present,* or *future* on the line following each sentence.

1. Rabbits are often called bunnies. _____

2. Rabbits were once classified as rodents. _____

3. Most rabbits live in a shallow hole called a form. _____

4. Most rabbits sleep during the day and eat from dusk to dawn. _____

5. Unfortunately, someone had the idea that rabbits might be tasty food. _____

6. Rabbits are near the bottom of the food chain. _____

7. Many people know that these lovely animals make good pets. _____

8. Each bunny has his or her own personality. _____

9. Watching a bunny's antics will make you laugh. _____

10. Perhaps someday rabbits will be enjoyed more as pets, not food. _____

STOP

29

Name _____ Date _____

Language Arts
2.E

Spelling Skills

Grammar and Usage of the English Language

Examples:

Find the word that is spelled correctly and fits best in the sentence.

A. The boat _____ toward shore.
- Ⓐ driffed
- Ⓑ drifded
- Ⓒ drifted
- Ⓓ drifteded

Answer: Ⓒ

One of the underlined words is misspelled. Which answer choice is spelled incorrectly?

B.
- Ⓕ great honor
- Ⓖ ackward moment
- Ⓗ bald eagle
- Ⓙ dark alley

Answer: Ⓖ

Read the directions carefully. Be sure you know if you should look for the correctly spelled word or the incorrectly spelled word.

DIRECTIONS: Find the word that is spelled correctly and fits best in the sentence.

1. _____ of the dog!
   - Ⓐ Beaware
   - Ⓑ Beware
   - Ⓒ Bewear
   - Ⓓ Bewaar

2. The _____ hit the moon.
   - Ⓕ asteroid
   - Ⓖ astroid
   - Ⓗ asterood
   - Ⓙ asteruod

3. He spoke with a _____ accent.
   - Ⓐ gutteral
   - Ⓑ gutterle
   - Ⓒ guttural
   - Ⓓ gutural

4. My favorite _____ is lemonade.
   - Ⓕ beaverage
   - Ⓖ beverage
   - Ⓗ bevirage
   - Ⓙ bevarage

5. The forest was _____ with color.
   - Ⓐ ablase
   - Ⓑ ableaze
   - Ⓒ ablaze
   - Ⓓ abblaze

DIRECTIONS: Read the phrases. Choose the phrase in which the underlined word is not spelled correctly.

6.
   - Ⓕ horizontle line
   - Ⓖ install software
   - Ⓗ graham cracker
   - Ⓙ firm mattress

7.
   - Ⓐ invisible man
   - Ⓑ covert operation
   - Ⓒ glove compartment
   - Ⓓ contagious disease

8.
   - Ⓕ our forfathers
   - Ⓖ burlap sack
   - Ⓗ hither and yon
   - Ⓙ graduating senior

Name _____   Date _____

DIRECTIONS: Read each answer. Fill in the space for the choice that has a spelling error. If there are no mistakes, fill in the last answer choice.

9.
   - Ⓐ veer
   - Ⓑ usher
   - Ⓒ surplus
   - Ⓓ No mistakes

10.
    - Ⓕ smack
    - Ⓖ stitch
    - Ⓗ toppel
    - Ⓙ No mistakes

11.
    - Ⓐ patter
    - Ⓑ schedulle
    - Ⓒ mute
    - Ⓓ No mistakes

DIRECTIONS: Read each phrase. One of the underlined words is not spelled correctly for the way it is used in the phrase. Fill in the circle for the word that is not spelled correctly.

12.
    - Ⓕ a flare for fashion
    - Ⓖ bottle cork
    - Ⓗ hunker down
    - Ⓙ internal medicine

13.
    - Ⓐ sentence fragment
    - Ⓑ the earth's corps
    - Ⓒ cancel an appointment
    - Ⓓ leaky faucet

14.
    - Ⓕ subtle hint
    - Ⓖ sensible plan
    - Ⓗ except an offer
    - Ⓙ food staples

DIRECTIONS: Find the word that is misspelled. If all the words are spelled correctly, fill in the circle for "No mistakes."

15. The abilitie to read is a vital skill for all.
        Ⓐ   Ⓑ Ⓒ

    No mistakes.
    Ⓓ

16. The surly usher sneered at the boy.
        Ⓕ   Ⓖ   Ⓗ

    No mistakes.
    Ⓙ

17. Dr. McCoy played billiards in the
                  Ⓐ

    lounge with a formidable opponent.
       Ⓑ   Ⓒ

    No mistakes.
    Ⓓ

18. The abbot in the abbie sings alto.
        Ⓕ   Ⓖ   Ⓗ

    No mistakes.
    Ⓙ

Name _____ Date _____

Language Arts

2.E

Spelling Correctly

Grammar and Usage of the English Language

DIRECTIONS: Fill in the blank with the word that best fits each sentence.

1. No one wanted to _____ the book with the wrinkled cover.

    by, buy

2. The cost of the newspaper has increased to seventy-five _____.

    cents, sense

3. Jamal, the social studies report is _____ tomorrow!

    do, dew, due

4. Call me when _____ my turn to use the computer.

    it's, its

5. We can rest when _____ is nothing left to put away.

    their, there, they're

6. The keys were _____ on the table this morning.

    here, hear

7. We'll get tickets when _____ in town next year.

    their, there, they're

8. Nathan _____ a chapter of the book every day after dinner.

    red, read

9. Aunt Jess _____ the package to me on Monday.

    sent, cent, scent

10. The car is parked in _____ usual space.

    it's, its

11. Chad and Greg brought _____ younger brother to the meeting.

    their, there, they're

12. Turner watched the catcher's sign, then _____ a perfect curve ball.

    threw, through

13. Nikki _____ the class in singing the national anthem.

    led, lead

14. Show Brendan _____ we keep the extra towels.

    where, wear

15. Put _____ backpack on the shelf by the door.

    your, you're

16. _____ going to be here any minute!

    Their, There, They're

17. I can't believe _____ time to go already.

    it's, its

18. Remember, _____ responsible for returning the videos.

    your, you're

32

Language Arts

2.F

Revising

Grammar and Usage of the English Language

DIRECTIONS: Answer the questions based on the passage below.

(1) Kerry was always wary of his brother: listening for footsteps or watching for flying objects such as books, toys, or sticks. (2) Once it was a large platter of pancakes. (3) Kerry had to keep his eyes open. (4) He also had to keep his ears open at all times. (5) Although Kerry and Jimmy were only a year apart, the boys were as different as Laurel and Hardy or Fred and Barney. (6) Jimmy, the older brother, was in seventh grade and was already six-feet tall and weighed 180 pounds. (7) But his mom loved him and thought he was a good boy.

(8) Jimmy was especially frightening today because he had a temper, which was large to match his size. (9) Today was the day of the annual race competition between the sixth and seventh graders. (10) The sixth graders were sure to win. (11) What Kerry lacked in size, he made up for in speed. (12) He was the fastest runner in the school. (13) And that was the problem. (14) Jimmy would be furious.

1. How are sentences 3 and 4 best combined?
   - (A) Kerry had to keep his eyes open, and he had to keep his ears open at all times.
   - (B) At all times, Kerry had to keep open his eyes and his ears also.
   - (C) Kerry at all times had to keep his eyes open and his ears also.
   - (D) Kerry had to keep his eyes and ears open at all times.

2. Which sentence does not belong in this story?
   - (F) Sentence 2
   - (G) Sentence 7
   - (H) Sentence 8
   - (J) Sentence 14

3. How is sentence 8 best written?
   - (A) Jimmy had a temper to match his size, which made him especially frightening today.
   - (B) Like his large size, Jimmy's temper was also large today, which made him especially frightening.
   - (C) Jimmy had a large temper and a large size, which made him especially frightening today.
   - (D) Today Jimmy had a temper, which was large to match his size, and he was especially frightening.

Name _____   Date _____

Language Arts

2.G

Revising by Rearranging

Grammar and Usage of the English Language

DIRECTIONS: Read about one town's centennial celebration. Use the story to answer questions 1–4.

> (1) We made a lot of preparations. (2) A cleanup committee washed all public buildings. (3) They also brushed all public buildings. (4) Members of the fire department climbed on high ladders to hang up flags and bunting. (5) Last May, our town celebrated its centennial anniversary.
>
> (6) At last, the celebration began. (7) The high point was when Mayor Lopez asked Olga Janssen—at 105, our oldest citizen—what she remembered about the old days. (8) Mrs. Janssen recalled how her mother had used a churn to make butter, and her favorite memory was of playing dominoes with her cousins.
>
> (9) At the end, we all drank a ginger ale toast to the town's next century. (10) We knew most of us would not be here for the next celebration, but we felt happy to be at this one. (11) A large bell was struck with a mallet by the mayor to officially close our celebration.

1. How would you revise the first paragraph to make it read more clearly?
   - Ⓐ Make the last sentence the first sentence.
   - Ⓑ Switch Sentence 1 with Sentence 2.
   - Ⓒ Delete Sentence 5.
   - Ⓓ Switch Sentence 1 with Sentence 4.

2. How are sentences 2 and 3 best combined?
   - Ⓕ A cleanup committee washed all public buildings and then brushed them.
   - Ⓖ A cleanup committee washed, and they also brushed, all public buildings.
   - Ⓗ A cleanup committee washed and brushed all public buildings.
   - Ⓙ As it is

3. How is sentence 11 best written?
   - Ⓐ The mayor officially closed our celebration with a mallet by striking a large bell.
   - Ⓑ Striking a large bell with a mallet, our celebration officially closed by the mayor.
   - Ⓒ To officially close our celebration, the mayor struck a large bell with a mallet.
   - Ⓓ As it is

4. Which sentence should be broken into two sentences?
   - Ⓕ 2
   - Ⓖ 5
   - Ⓗ 8
   - Ⓙ 10

34

Name _____ Date _____

DIRECTIONS: For numbers 5–7, choose the answer that best combines the sentences.

5. **Mr. Norton called this morning.**
   Mr. Norton said his wife is sick.
   - (A) Mr. Norton called this morning and Mr. Norton said his wife is sick.
   - (B) Mr. Norton called this morning, and he said his wife is sick.
   - (C) This morning, Mr. Norton called and said his wife is sick.
   - (D) Mr. Norton called this morning to say his wife is sick.

6. **George left early.**
   Carol left early.
   They are going to the band festival.
   - (F) George and Carol left early because to the band festival they are going.
   - (G) George and Carol left early to go to the band festival.
   - (H) George left early and Carol because they are going to the band festival.
   - (J) Leaving early, George and Carol are going to the band festival.

7. **The birds sing beautifully.**
   The birds are in the tree.
   - (A) The birds are in the tree, and they sing beautifully.
   - (B) The birds, in the tree, singing beautifully.
   - (C) The birds sing beautifully and are in the tree.
   - (D) The birds in the tree sing beautifully.

DIRECTIONS: For numbers 8 and 9, choose the best way of expressing the idea.

8.
   - (F) Because year after year, the salmon struggle upstream to spawn.
   - (G) Upstream to spawn, the salmon struggle year after year.
   - (H) Year after year, the salmon struggle upstream to spawn.
   - (J) The salmon struggle year after year upstream to spawn.

9.
   - (A) The plumber fixed the pipe because it was leaking.
   - (B) The plumber fixed the leaking pipe.
   - (C) Because the pipe was leaking, the plumber fixed the pipe.
   - (D) The pipe was leaking, and the plumber fixed the pipe.

STOP

Name _____   Date _____

Language Arts

2.H

Revising by Adding or Deleting

Grammar and Usage of the English Language

DIRECTIONS: For numbers 1 and 2, read the paragraph. Find the sentence that does not belong in the paragraph.

1. (1) Canada is more than a land of great beauty. (2) It borders the United States to the south. (3) It is also a land of vast forests. (4) Lumber and the products that come from lumber make Canada a leader in world paper production. (5) The pulp and paper industry continues to grow and is now Canada's leading industry.

   Ⓐ Sentence 2
   Ⓑ Sentence 3
   Ⓒ Sentence 4
   Ⓓ Sentence 5

2. (1) The most beautiful of all horses is the Arabian Asil. (2) Its neck is gracefully arched. (3) Its head is small and delicate with eyes that are large, fiery, and far apart. (4) Its small ears point inward. (5) This horse is well noted for its endurance. (6) The horse has a full, flowing tail, and its skin is a shiny black.

   Ⓕ Sentence 2
   Ⓖ Sentence 4
   Ⓗ Sentence 5
   Ⓙ Sentence 6

DIRECTIONS: For numbers 3 and 4, read the paragraph. Find the sentence that best fits the blank in the paragraph.

3. He was greeted by enthusiastic crowds in Paris and London. When he returned to the United States, he was given one of the largest ticker-tape parades in New York history. Overnight, his name became a household word. _____. Aviator Douglas Corrigan, who, following a most unusual feat, was known worldwide as Wrong-Way Corrigan.

   Ⓐ Whether it was legitimate or not, Douglas Corrigan's flight made him famous.
   Ⓑ His ideas were as well known as the President's.
   Ⓒ Who was this new American hero?
   Ⓓ Where did this man call his home?

4. In 1937, Douglas Corrigan had requested permission to fly over the Atlantic to Europe. His request was denied after federal aviation officials inspected his plane. _____. One tank was even located directly in front of the pilot's seat and nearly blocked Corrigan's vision.

   Ⓕ His plane did not have the capacity to hold enough fuel to cross the ocean.
   Ⓖ Corrigan had added so many extra gas tanks to his dilapidated craft that it was considered a deathtrap.
   Ⓗ Authorities feared Corrigan would run out of fuel with no land in sight.
   Ⓙ His plane had no added room for extra supplies of food and water.

Name _____   Date _____

DIRECTIONS: Read this story about Amelia Earhart. Use the story to answer questions 5–8.

(1) <u>The weather was bad</u> over the mid-Atlantic Ocean. (2) The small plane's engine sputtered. (3) The slim, young woman at the controls knew she was too far out to turn back. (4) Carefully, she coaxed the plane ahead through the storm.

(5) When dawn came, the engine was failing seriously. (6) Just ahead lay the Irish coast. (7) As the engine gasped its last breath, the woman brought her plane down in a cow pasture. (8) An astonished farmer raced over as the young woman climbed out of the airplane. (9) "I'm from America," she said. (10) "My name is Amelia Earhart." (11) The farmer was angry that she had ruined part of his field. (12) She had even set a new speed record: thirteen hours and thirty minutes!

(13) They didn't think a woman was strong enough to keep going through the long night. (14) However, Earhart had strength and courage to spare. (15) She had already made parachute jumps and had explored the ocean floor in a diver's suit. (16) Now, overnight, she had become famous.

5. Which sentence could be added after sentence 10?
   - (A) The farmer thought she was an alien from outer space.
   - (B) She had become the first woman to fly over the Atlantic Ocean alone.
   - (C) She had become the first woman to safely land in a pasture.
   - (D) She added, "Do you know where I might get something good to eat?"

6. Which sentence could begin the third paragraph?
   - (F) Many people had told Amelia not to make this flight.
   - (G) Amelia wanted to give up.
   - (H) Amelia was a weak woman.
   - (J) Amelia loved to set world records.

7. Which group of words would be more colorful than the underlined words in sentence 1?
   - (A) There was lightning
   - (B) Lightning ripped through the blackness
   - (C) It was cold and wet
   - (D) The weather was stormy

8. Which sentence does not belong in the story?
   - (F) Sentence 2
   - (G) Sentence 6
   - (H) Sentence 11
   - (J) Sentence 16

Name _____ Date _____

Language Arts

2.1

Using Reference Books

Grammar and Usage of the English Language

DIRECTIONS: Look at the picture of the set of encyclopedias. Each encyclopedia is numbered and contains information about topics that begin with the letters shown on the volume.

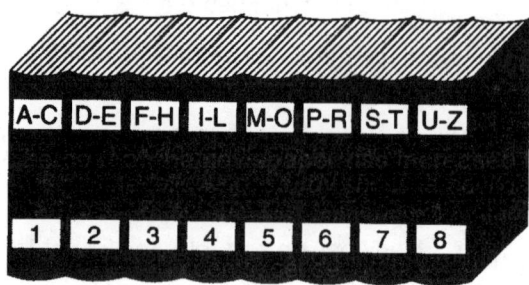

1. Which of these topics would be found in Volume 5?
   - (A) goats
   - (B) nursing
   - (C) a biography of Neil Armstrong
   - (D) the history of Canada

2. In which volume would you find information on dinosaurs?
   - (F) Volume 2
   - (G) Volume 4
   - (H) Volume 6
   - (J) Volume 7

3. Which of these topics would not be found in Volume 1?
   - (A) the game of basketball
   - (B) a biography of Hans Christian Andersen
   - (C) animals
   - (D) a biography of Colin Powell

4. In which volume would you find a map of the United States?
   - (F) Volume 1
   - (G) Volume 3
   - (H) Volume 6
   - (J) Volume 8

DIRECTIONS: Read each question below. Fill in the circle next to the correct answer.

5. Look at these guide words from a dictionary page.
   era—everyday
   Which word could be found on the page?
   - (A) evict
   - (B) entire
   - (C) eternal
   - (D) equipment

6. Look at these guide words from a dictionary page.
   license—local
   Which word could be found on the page?
   - (F) locate
   - (G) light
   - (H) liberty
   - (J) logical

7. Which of these is a main heading that includes the other three words?
   - (A) Fruits
   - (B) Grapes
   - (C) Oranges
   - (D) Strawberries

8. Which of these is a main heading that includes the other three words?
   - (F) Oxygen
   - (G) Helium
   - (H) Hydrogen
   - (J) Gases

Name _____ Date _____

Language Arts
2.0
For pages 21–38

Mini-Test 2

Grammar and Usage of the English Language

DIRECTIONS: Read the passage. Choose the best answer to each question.

    The practice of wearing rings is a very ancient one. Throughout history, people in many lands have decorated their bodies by wearing rings on their fingers, ears, lips, necks, noses, ankles, and wrists. In some cultures, a married woman wore a ring on the big toe of her left foot; a man might have put rings on his second and third toes. Today, the practice of wearing rings in some cases includes multiple facial rings, as well as rings in many other areas of the body.

1. What is the paragraph mainly about?
   - (A) why some people wore rings on their toes
   - (B) what kinds of rings were the most popular
   - (C) when the practice of wearing rings began
   - (D) how people throughout history have worn rings

2. Which title best summarizes this passage?
   - (F) *Rings Worn Today*
   - (G) *Rings Throughout the Ages*
   - (H) *Rings in Unusual Places*
   - (J) *Rings Are Fun*

DIRECTIONS: Choose the punctuation mark that is needed in the sentence. If no punctuation is needed, choose "None of the above."

3. "That was great" exclaimed Stephen.
   - (A) !
   - (B) .
   - (C) ,
   - (D) None of the above

4. We have band on Monday Wednesday, and Friday.
   - (F) ;
   - (G) ,
   - (H) :
   - (J) None of the above

5. He said he wanted to go home now.
   - (A) ,
   - (B) :
   - (C) "
   - (D) None of the above

6. "When can we leave? Nate inquired.
   - (F) ,
   - (G) "
   - (H) :
   - (J) None of the above

7. Her list included the following clean room, do dishes, feed dog.
   - (A) ,
   - (B) :
   - (C) ;
   - (D) None of the above

GO →

DIRECTIONS: Find the word that is spelled correctly and fits best in the blank.

8. Do not _____ the barrier.
   - (F) crossing
   - (G) crossed
   - (H) cross
   - (J) crosses

9. My mother _____ to shop for antiques.
   - (A) love
   - (B) loving
   - (C) lovely
   - (D) loves

10. Do you have any _____ foil?
    - (F) alluminum
    - (G) aluminum
    - (H) alloominem
    - (J) aluminem

11. He was very _____.
    - (A) purplexed
    - (B) purplecked
    - (C) perplexed
    - (D) perplecked

12. My brother has to use an inhaler for his _____.
    - (F) asma
    - (G) asthma
    - (H) asthme
    - (J) ashma

DIRECTIONS: Use the paragraph below to answer the questions.

(1) "This is a pretty good poem," she thought to herself. (2) "It's just that . . . " (3) Lois wondered if she had fed her dog before she left for school. (4) Then, her name was called, she stood up, and her knees began to shake. (5) When she turned around and looked at the rest of the class, however, she saw friendly faces.

13. Choose the best first sentence for this paragraph.
    - (A) Lois waited for her turn to read her poem in front of the class.
    - (B) Lois could hardly wait to go to lunch.
    - (C) Lois was looking forward to reading her play.
    - (D) Lois loved English class.

14. Which sentence should be left out of this paragraph?
    - (F) Sentence 1
    - (G) Sentence 2
    - (H) Sentence 3
    - (J) Sentence 5

15. Choose the last sentence for this paragraph.
    - (A) "Oh, no," she remembered, "I didn't feed the dog."
    - (B) Lois felt like running from the room.
    - (C) Lois decided that this would be a great time to read all of her poems.
    - (D) "Maybe this won't be so bad after all," Lois thought with relief.

Language Arts Standards

3.0 Literature
Using the literature read during the school year, students should be able to:

3.A Identify and compare similar themes in a variety of books. *(See page 42.)*

3.B Notice and think about the way descriptive language (for example, simile, metaphor, personification) helps an author create meaning. *(See pages 43–45.)*

What it means:
Descriptive language is used for descriptive effect. It describes or implies meaning, rather than directly stating it. Examples of descriptive language include:
- **similes**—using *like* or *as* to compare things that may seem unlike each other. Example: Her smile was as dazzling as the sun.
- **metaphors**—comparing unlike things but without using *like* or *as*. Example: His body was a well-oiled machine.
- **personification**—assigning human qualities, feelings, or actions to an animal, an object, or an idea. Example: The mother bear cried for her cub.

3.C Identify and compare literary elements (for example, setting, plot, character, rhythm, rhyme) in different types of literature. *(See pages 46–51.)*

3.D Examine the ways in which characters change and develop throughout a story. *(See pages 52–53.)*

3.E Develop and compare ideas (for example, draw conclusions, make predictions) about events, characters, and settings from one book to another. *(See pages 54–55.)*

3.F Produce written work in at least one literary genre (e.g., poetry).

Name _____ Date _____

Language Arts   **Literature**

3.A

Comparing Books

DIRECTIONS: What do you like to read? From the library, choose four books that have a similar theme. Read them and write a brief summary of each.

1. Title: _____

   Summary: _____
   _____
   _____
   _____
   _____

2. Title: _____

   Summary: _____
   _____
   _____
   _____
   _____

3. Title: _____

   Summary: _____
   _____
   _____
   _____
   _____

4. Title: _____

   Summary: _____
   _____
   _____
   _____
   _____

5. What is the similar theme of the books you chose?

   _____
   _____
   _____
   _____

6. What are the main differences in the books you chose?

   _____
   _____
   _____
   _____
   _____

7. In what ways are the books you chose the same?

   _____
   _____
   _____
   _____
   _____

8. Which type of book did you like the most? Why?

   _____
   _____
   _____
   _____
   _____

STOP

Name _____ Date _____

Language Arts
3.B Literature

Similes and Metaphors

DIRECTIONS: Read the story. Then, answer the questions on the next page.

Sollie, the Rock

I've lived on a lake for most of my life. I've had lots of time to learn all sorts of fun things to do in the water. I think my favorite thing of all is waterskiing. That's why I decided to invite my best friend, Sollie, over to give it a try.

Sollie had never been on skis before, but I knew Dad could help him learn, just like he helped me.

Waterskiing is like flying. If you aren't afraid of getting up, you'll enjoy the ride. That's what I told Sollie before we spent the afternoon trying to get him up on skis for the first time.

I thought it would be easy. Sollie is a seal, sleek and smooth in the water, bobbing in and out

of the waves. I thought someone so agile would find skiing easy. It didn't dawn on me until the fourth try that Sollie is shaped more like a rock than a bird.

On his first try, Sollie let go of the towrope when Dad hit the gas. He sank as fast as the *Titanic*. The only things visible were the tips of his skis.

On his second try, Sollie leaned into the skis, flipping head over heels like a gymnast falling off the balance beam. His skis formed an "X" that marked the spot where he disappeared.

On the third try, Sollie stood up. He teetered forward and then back, as if he were a rag doll. His biggest mistake was holding on to the rope after he lost both skis. He flopped about behind the boat like a giant carp until he finally let go.

On the fourth try, Sollie bent his knees, straightened his back, and flew around the lake behind the boat as if he were a professional skier. He jumped the wake, rolled out next to the boat, and waved at me. He was "the man."

After three times around the lake, Sollie let go of the rope. He returned to his former self and dropped into the water like a rock.

After spending the afternoon out on the water with Dad and me, Sollie fell in love with waterskiing. We made plans to do it again soon. Maybe even a rock can learn to fly!

GO ➡

43

Name _____ Date _____

> **Examples:**
>
> A **metaphor** is a direct comparison between two unlike things.
>   Example: Bobby is a mouse.
>
> A **simile** is an indirect comparison between two unlike things using the words *like, as,* or *as if* to make the comparison.
>   Example: Bobby is like a mouse.

1. Identify the following lines as metaphors or similes.

    _____ Sollie is a seal, sleek and smooth in the water, bobbing in and out of the waves.

    _____ Sollie is shaped more like a rock than a bird.

    _____ He sank as fast as the *Titanic*.

    _____ He flopped about behind the boat like a giant carp until he finally let go.

2. What do the above similes suggest about Sollie?

    _____

    _____

3. Why is the following sentence not a simile or a metaphor?

    Sollie bent his knees, straightened his back, and flew around the lake behind the boat as if he were a professional skier.

    - (A) It does not make a comparison.
    - (B) It makes a comparison between like things.
    - (C) It makes a contrast rather than a comparison.
    - (D) The comparison is not between a person and an animal.

4. Fill in the blank to turn the sentence into a simile.

    Sollie bent his knees, straightened his back, and flew around the lake behind the boat

    _____

    _____

    _____ .

5. If the story's title were changed from *Sollie, the Rock* to *Sollie, the Bird,* how do you think the story would have been different?

    _____

    _____

    _____

Name _____ Date _____

Language Arts

3.B

Personification

Literature

DIRECTIONS: Read the passage and answer the questions that follow.

> **Autumn Dance**
>
> Every October, autumn bullies summer into letting go of the skies. The wind breathes a chill into the air. The sun gets tired and goes to bed earlier each night, and night sleeps in later each day. The trees dress in bright gowns for the last celebration of the season, and the leaves are skipping and dancing down the sidewalk. This is autumn, standing firm with hands on her hips, until winter peers over the edge of the world.

1. This passage tells about _____ .
   - (A) winter turning into spring
   - (B) fall turning into winter
   - (C) spring turning into summer
   - (D) summer turning into fall

2. How does the sun change during autumn?
   - (F) It rises and sets earlier than in the summer.
   - (G) It rises and sets later than in the summer.
   - (H) It rises later but sets earlier than in the summer.
   - (J) It rises earlier but sets later than in the summer.

3. What is the author referring to when she describes the trees dressed in "bright gowns"?
   - (A) leaves that have changed color but have not yet fallen from the trees
   - (B) green leaves
   - (C) formal dresses
   - (D) the trees' empty branches

4. Personification means giving human qualities to animals or objects. Which sentence is not an example of personification?
   - (F) Every October, autumn bullies summer into letting go of the skies.
   - (G) A cold wind blows.
   - (H) The leaves skipped and danced down the sidewalk.
   - (J) The sun gets tired and goes to bed.

STOP

45

Name _____ Date _____

Language Arts

3.C

Analyzing Characters

Literature

DIRECTIONS: Read the story. Then, answer the questions on the next page.

Slumber Party

It was the night Annabel had looked forward to for weeks. Four girls were arriving for a sleepover party! She had asked her parents many times, and finally they said *yes.* Annabel nervously wandered around the house, waiting for her guests to arrive. Finally, four cars pulled up and the doorbell rang.

Annabel threw open the door and welcomed her guests. The girls piled into Annabel's house in a jumble of sleeping bags and overnight cases.

"Thank you for inviting me," Robin said. "I brought you a thank-you gift." She held a small box out to her hostess.

"Yum! Chocolates!" Sheila shouted. She grabbed the box and shoved a candy into her mouth. She dropped the empty wrapper on the floor. "Got any milk?" she said with her mouth full.

"There's milk in the kitchen," Annabel said as she pointed the way. Then, she noticed that another one of her guests did not look happy. "Tamiko, what's wrong?"

"I've never slept away from home," Tamiko admitted. "I'm a little nervous. My mother said I could call home if I needed to."

"You'll be all right," Annabel reassured her. "But, you can use the phone anytime. It's right over there . . . hey? Where's the phone?" She looked at the empty table. Her eyes followed the telephone cord to a corner of the room. A girl was talking animatedly into the phone. It was the last guest, Paula.

"Is it okay if my friend Dan comes over?" Paula called over to Annabel. "He says he's bored."

"No!" Annabel responded, a little shocked. "There are no boys at this slumber party. Well, except for my kid brother, Ted."

"Oh." Paula rolled her eyes and went back to chatting on the phone.

"I brought a flashlight and a teddy bear," Tamiko showed the girls. "They'll help me feel better in the middle of the night."

"I'll put my sleeping bag next to yours," Robin told her. "I hope that makes you feel safer."

"Don't worry," Annabel smiled. "There's nothing to be afraid of!"

"Oh, yeah?" Ted chuckled to himself from his hiding place at the top of the staircase. Annabel's brother was wearing a horrible monster mask, and he carried a plastic ax. "Just wait until I jump into their room at midnight!"

 GO

46

Name _____ Date _____

DIRECTIONS: Pick a word from the Word Bank to describe each of the characters. Write two examples from the story that prove why your description fits each person.

Word Bank		
fearful	greedy	polite
gracious	mischievous	rude

Example:

Annabel is <u>gracious</u>.
- A. She says "Welcome!" to her guests.
- B. She shows her friends where the milk and the phone are when she's asked.

1. Robin is _____.

   A. _____
      _____
   B. _____
      _____

2. Sheila is _____.

   A. _____
      _____
   B. _____
      _____

3. Tamiko is _____.

   A. _____
      _____
   B. _____
      _____

4. Paula is _____.

   A. _____
      _____
   B. _____
      _____

5. Ted is _____.

   A. _____
      _____
   B. _____
      _____

STOP

Name _____   Date _____

Language Arts

3.C

Analyzing Setting

Literature

DIRECTIONS: Read the story. Then, complete the activity on the next page.

Summer Camp

Our camp is great. A bunch of kids from school go there, but I especially like meeting kids from other schools. We sing crazy songs in the dining hall everyday at noon. There are activities and challenges to try all day long. The counselors are great, the buildings are clean and airy, and the food is better than some meals I eat at home.

This year, Keesha is my counselor. She is so funny! She gets all us girls rolling on the cabin floor laughing at her silly, scary stories at bedtime. But she is smart, too. She knows when one of us is homesick or feels bad. She never pokes fun at us when we do something stupid, and she shows us how to express kindness to the others in our cabin. Keesha loves nature. She often points out the wildlife in camp. On our second morning of camp, Keesha raced outside as if there were a bee down her back. She yelled something about the witching hour. I always thought that the witching hour was at midnight. We all thought she had gone off the deep end. Keesha rushed over to a beech tree. The elephant-like trunk had a big hole in it where a woodpecker had hammered out a home. Our counselor reached her hands into the hole and pulled out a young possum. It chittered and squeaked until it saw us. Then, it pretended to be asleep!

One night, she took all ten of us for a hike through the woods. She warned us to be quiet and to leave our flashlights at the cabin. We walked for twenty minutes when we stopped suddenly. We heard chattering creatures off to our right. Down by the lake, two raccoons were fighting over some bread. They sounded like two children squabbling over a treat.

One rainy day, we chose to go deep into the state forest with binoculars, guidebooks, insect repellent, and snack food. We sketched some of the wonderful flowering plants. Keesha knew the history and medicinal value of many of these plants. She showed us one plant that, when broken open, gave off a very powerful smell. She told us it would keep flies and mosquitoes away. I sure understood why the plant would work!

Every evening after supper, we'd play games with a group of kids from other cabins. Keesha volunteered my bunkmates and me to set up the evening game on our fifth day. We walked all over the camp, setting clues for a treasure hunt. This meant that we had to canoe to different landmarks around the lake, crawl under some of the older cabins, plan obscure hiding spots "that everyone should have known about," and race down the camp trails. Of course, we ran out of time. When the bell rang for supper, we were still far across the field.

In our giggle-filled dash to the dining hall, we waded through some tall grass. My new friend, Rita, unknowingly stepped over a light blue-gray snake. It was huge! Keesha said it was a blue racer. We all stood back and watched it, talking quietly. "Look how long it is," said Keesha. "It must be as long as I am!" We watched as the startled snake started to move slowly past us and then suddenly raced away. We were late for supper that day, but it didn't matter.

I want to go back to camp next summer. I want to know as much about nature as Keesha does. I can dream, can't I?

GO ▶

Name _____ Date _____

1. List the two main elements of the setting.

    Time: _____

    Place: _____

2. Match the specific setting elements with these events by drawing lines to connect.

EVENT	PLACE	TIME
see baby possum	in field	every noon
sing songs	by beech tree	rainy day
discover blue racer	in woods	bedtime
sketch plant specimens	in dining hall	second day
hear scary stories	in state forest	one night
observe raccoons	in cabin	fifth day

3. Describe the summer camp by discussing the various activities of the campers.

_____
_____
_____
_____
_____
_____
_____
_____
_____
_____
_____
_____

STOP

Name _____ Date _____

Language Arts
3.C

Setting and Plot

Literature

DIRECTIONS: Read each passage. Then, answer the questions.

The space taxi's engine hummed. Nathan's teeth chattered. Little wells of moisture beaded up on his forehead and palms. *I can't fly,* he thought. *Mars is just around the corner, but it's still too far to be stuck in this taxi.* Nathan knew that his uncle was waiting for him, waiting for help with his hydroponic farm. At first, that didn't matter. In his mind, Nathan saw himself leaping out of his seat and bolting toward the door. But then he thought of his uncle. Nathan knew that if he did not help his uncle, the crops he had worked so hard to nurture and grow would not be ready for the Mars 3 season. He took a deep breath and settled back for the remainder of the flight. He couldn't wait to see the look on his uncle's face when he stepped off the taxi.

1. What is the setting of this story?

   Ⓐ Earth
   Ⓑ a space farm
   Ⓒ a space taxi
   Ⓓ unknown

2. What is this story's plot?

   Ⓕ Nathan's uncle has asked him to come to Mars.
   Ⓖ Nathan was afraid he would fall asleep in the taxi and miss his stop.
   Ⓗ Nathan doesn't like to work on a hydroponic farm.
   Ⓙ Nathan had to overcome his fear of flying to help his uncle.

"What do you wanna play?" Will asked as he shoved a bite of pancake into his mouth.

"*Scramble.* We are *Scramble* maniacs at this house," said Scott.

Will poured more orange juice into his glass. "How about that game where you ask dumb questions about stuff everyone always forgets?"

"*Trivial Questions,*" said Scott.

"Yeah, that's it."

"Can you name the seven dwarfs?" asked Eric.

"Snoopy, Sneezy, Dopey," said Scott.

"Nah, Snoopy's a dog," said Eric.

"Let's do something else," Will chimed in as he cut his pancake in half.

"Let's play *Scramble,*" said Scott.

"That's too much like school. Let's play football," said Eric.

"It's too cold out," said Scott.

"Let's dig out your connector sets. I haven't played with those for years," Eric said as he pushed his chair back and stood.

"Yeah," said Scott and Will as they jumped from their seats.

3. What is the setting for this story?

   Ⓐ Scott's bedroom
   Ⓑ Scott's living room
   Ⓒ Scott's kitchen
   Ⓓ Scott's basement

4. What is this story's plot?

   Ⓕ The boys cannot remember the names of the seven dwarfs.
   Ⓖ The boys cannot decide what they want to do.
   Ⓗ The boys do not want to play *Scramble.*
   Ⓙ It's too cold to play football.

50

Name _____ Date _____

Language Arts　　　　　　　　　　　　　　　　　　　　　　　Literature

3.C
Using Rhyme

DIRECTIONS: Poets who set up a pattern of rhymes at the end of each line are creating a **rhyme scheme.** In a rhyme scheme, the first line is designated *a,* and all lines that rhyme with that word are also designated *a.* If the next line does not rhyme with the first, it is designated with a *b.*

> **Example:**
>
> Each day I walk to school and see *(a)*
> A lot of people driving cars. *(b)*
> Why don't they choose to walk, like me? *(a)*

By the Ocean

As she walked along the sandy shore　　_____
with delight as nature's wonders she did see　_____
starfish, whitecaps, conch shells, and more.　_____
She knew that she would never fly free　_____
like the tissue-paper seagulls above　_____
or swim with the dolphins she did love.　_____

1. At the end of each line, label the "By the Ocean" poem with the correct rhyme scheme. Then, fill in the following chart by placing words that rhyme together.

a	b	c

2. Make a list of your own rhyming words about the ocean. Use them as a starting point for writing a poem.

_____

_____

_____

Name _____ Date _____

Language Arts

3.D

Examining Character Development

Literature

DIRECTIONS: Read the story. Then, fill in the character webs with words that describe the characters.

Go, Man, Go!

They stretched in midfield, preparing for the morning's events. Theo, dressed in the red and white of his school, worked alongside the rest of the seventeen athletes who had come to the meet from Weston Middle School.

Theo was hardworking, and he had trained well. Since the snow thawed in early March, he had kept his disciplined regiments of warm-up, long run, sprints, and cool-down. As the weeks passed, he settled into a daily four-mile run. The first few times were painful. His side ached, his calves tightened, his right knee flared, and his forehead burned. On those nights, he would flop down on his bed and sleep soundly without even undressing.

Now, on this warm and bright May morning, it was time to prove his worth, and Theo found he was very nervous. Twenty-two schools were participating in the invitational meet. The field was spangled with athletes whose school-colored clothes offered a visual display of diversity. Weston's girls had already scored points in the long jump and javelin. The boys had done well, too. Theo's high jump had won his school a second place. They also had a second and fourth in the pole vault. Not bad, considering that track and field was a brand new sport to Weston Middle School.

Theo's main event was the 400-meter dash. It was what he dreamed of running ever since he saw his Uncle Dave's victorious sprint seven years ago. Yet, these meets made Theo so nervous, he often wished he were sacked out in front of the television instead. As he pranced about, shaking away the jitters, Theo saw a lone figure at the long-jump pit. He was a thin, dark boy roughly Theo's height and build. He wore the only gray T-shirt in the wild mass of school colors. Even though he looked out of place, the boy seemed calm and sure of himself. Theo crossed over to the pit. He introduced himself to the runner, a friendly, determined student named Carl Alvarez. Carl was the only entrant from his school. He had taken two city buses to get there, and he was there just for the 400-meter race. Like Theo, this was his first year in track and field. Carl didn't seem fazed by his solitary status, though. He told Theo he wanted to help form a team at his school. Returning to his own gathered team, Theo admitted to himself that Carl's attitude was impressive.

When the 400 was announced and Theo lined up, the Weston team set up a chant. Theo glanced at Carl, who didn't have anyone to cheer for him, but Carl seemed focused and ready for his race. As the pistol fired, Theo shot out. The full field of runners—eight boys in eight lanes—swarmed down the stretch. The Weston team yelled, "Go, man, go!" Every Weston student screamed as Theo's lead became evident coming out of the first curve.

Theo's heart pounded as he crossed over to the inside lane. He was leading! Footsteps thudded behind him as he entered the wide, dangerous final turn. Someone was pulling alongside him. It was Carl! They glanced at each other briefly. Then they focused. Theo looked ahead and smiled grimly. Okay, let's race, he thought. Around the curve he ran, Carl at his side matching him step for step, yet never falling back. The two boys sped into the final stretch. Theo raced as never before, neck to neck with his challenger.

GO

52

Name _____ Date _____

Personality traits	— Theo —	How he feels before the race
		What he does during the race
		What he probably does to finish the race

Personality traits	— Carl —	How he feels before the race
		What he does during the race
		What he probably does to finish the race

STOP

Name _____ Date _____

Language Arts Literature

3.E

Drawing Conclusions

DIRECTIONS: Read each passage and answer the questions.

I'll admit the list is long. I broke Mom's favorite blue vase playing baseball in the house. It was a home run, but that didn't count much with Mom. I broke the back window. I didn't think I could break a window by shoving my hip against a door. It must have been bad glass. I ruined the living room carpet by leaving a red spot the size of a basketball. I know the rule—no drinking in the living room—but I wasn't really drinking. I didn't even get a sip before I dropped the glass.

I guess "Trouble" is my middle name. At least that's what Mom says. So, you won't be surprised when I tell you I'm in trouble once again.

1. What is the main problem in the story?

    A The narrator drinks red pop in the living room.
    B The narrator breaks and destroys things.
    C The narrator disobeys the rules.
    D The narrator is in trouble again.

2. What do you think happens next in the story?

    F The narrator gets a paper route to pay for all the damages.
    G The narrator apologizes for ruining the carpet.
    H The narrator tells about the latest trouble he caused.
    J The narrator asks for a new middle name.

Skip crossed only one set of fingers when he made a wish. He avoided black cats and never stepped on cracks in the sidewalk. He thought he was a perfect candidate to win something, anything.

Skip knew that winning took more than avoiding cracks and black cats. That's why he tried out for the track team. Skip wanted to hear the words, "You are the winner!" He imagined hearing his name announced over the loud speaker. However, Skip didn't work very hard at practice and didn't make the team.

Skip spent his free time kicking stones down the street. He pretended he was an NFL kicker in a championship game. The score was always 0–0, and his kick would cinch the title. In his imagination, he always scored.

Skip believed he would be a football star when he grew up. He decided it didn't matter that he hadn't made the track team. He would play football when he got to high school. He was such a great kicker, he would easily make the team. He might even play in college, he thought. He really wanted to be a winner.

3. Which sentence best summarizes this story?

    A Skip was very superstitious.
    B Skip really wanted to be a winner.
    C Skip had a vivid imagination.
    D Track was not the right sport for Skip.

4. Which sentence best describes what Skip will need to do to be a winner?

    F Skip will need to stop being so superstitious.
    G Skip will need to work hard to succeed.
    H Skip will need to find someone to coach him.
    J Skip will need to stop kicking stones.

Name _____ Date _____

Language Arts
3.E

Making Predictions

Literature

DIRECTIONS: Read the story. Then, fill in the chart below.

The Race Is On!

Lee and Kim are both running for class president. This is a big job. The president has to help organize special events for the class, such as environmental projects, holiday parties, visit-the-elderly outings, and field trips.

Lee has been campaigning for several weeks. He really wants to be elected president. He prepared a speech telling the class all of the great ideas he hopes to accomplish if he wins. For example, Lee wants to have a car-wash picnic to earn money for the homeless. He also wants to recycle aluminum cans to earn money for a field trip to the new Exploration Science Center. Lee has been working hard for this position.

Kim hasn't done much, if any, campaigning. She figures she has lots of friends who will vote for her. Instead of a speech, she gave a big pool party at her house. Kim believes the class should work to earn money, but she believes that any money they raise should be used for their class. Why give money to someone else when there are lots of great places to visit on field trips in their city?

The day of the big election arrives. The votes are in. The winner is . . .

1.

Reasons Lee Might Win	Reasons Kim Might Win

2. Who do you think will win? Why?

_____

_____

_____

STOP

55

Language Arts

3.0

For pages 42–55

Mini-Test 3

Literature

DIRECTIONS: Read the story. Then, answer the questions on the next page.

By Saturday Noon

Saturday noon is one of those special times in our house. When I say special, I don't mean good special. By Saturday noon, my sisters and I need to have our bedrooms pristine.

When Dad inspects our rooms, he is like an army sergeant doing the white-glove test. If anything is out of place, if any clothes are left on the floor, and if your dresser isn't cleaned off and shiny, you don't get to go anywhere that day.

That isn't hard for Margaret. She's a neat freak. But Chelsea and I are normal, which is the problem—two normal sisters sharing a bedroom. On Monday, we start our separate piles: dirty clothes, wrinkled clothes, clothes we decided not to wear but forgot to hang up. By Wednesday, it's hard to find the floor. By Friday, the tops of the dressers are loaded. Plus, Mom won't let us throw everything down the laundry chute. "Sort it," she says.

Usually, we have enough time to get our clothes all folded and hung by noon, but last Saturday, Chelsea got sick. She spent the morning in the bathroom. I was left to clean the room alone. I had plans to shop with Jen.

At 10:00, Jen decided she wanted to leave early. I was desperate, so I shoved everything under Chelsea's bed, dusted the dressers, plumped the pillows, and called Dad for a room check.

Dad started his checklist. Everything was okay until Dad got to my closet. He turned and asked, "Where are all your clothes, Sara?"

"Dirty," I confessed.

Dad looked around until he spied the clothes under Chelsea's bed. "Dirty?" he asked.

I winced. "I must have missed those."

"Call Jen. You're not going shopping today," he said.

By Saturday noon, I was sick right alongside Chelsea. Mom said, "It's a good thing you didn't go shopping."

I figured it was just the opposite. If I had gone shopping, I would never have gotten sick.

Name _____   Date _____

1. **The words in the title "Saturday Noon" are used three times in the story. Why is that time important to Sara?**
   - (A) Chelsea wanted to go shopping.
   - (B) It was the deadline for having her room clean, which determined whether or not she could go out that day.
   - (C) It was the time Sara had to have the laundry done.
   - (D) It was when she got sick.

2. **How is Margaret different from Sara and Chelsea?**
   - (F) She is older.
   - (G) She is younger.
   - (H) She is very neat.
   - (J) She always goes out on Saturdays.

3. **What is the setting of this story?**
   - (A) Sara's house
   - (B) the mall
   - (C) Chicago
   - (D) Margaret's room

4. **Which of the following is not one of Sara's excuses for not getting her room clean?**
   - (F) Sara's mom will not let her throw clothes down the laundry chute.
   - (G) Chelsea got sick and couldn't help.
   - (H) Jen wanted to leave early.
   - (J) Her mom should clean her room.

5. **What is this story's plot?**
   - (A) Sara can't wait to go shopping.
   - (B) Sara knows she needs to have her room clean by Saturday noon, but blames everyone but herself for her room not being clean.
   - (C) Sara allows her laundry to build up.
   - (D) Sara's dad has unrealistic expectations for Sara.

6. **Which title below best fits this story?**
   - (F) *The Blame Game*
   - (G) *Cleaning Is Not Normal*
   - (H) *Shopping With Jen*
   - (J) *Laundry Woes*

DIRECTIONS: Choose the best answer.

7. **Which of the following sentences includes a metaphor?**
   - (A) Janet was an accident waiting to happen.
   - (B) She watched the sun set in the orange sky.
   - (C) The young boy swam like a fish.
   - (D) The wind whispered through the trees.

8. **Which of the following sentences includes a simile?**
   - (F) Through the whole tragedy, Michael was a rock.
   - (G) She liked the warmth of the sun on her face.
   - (H) Mallory said, "You're as sharp as a tack."
   - (J) Please look like you want to be here.

9. **Which of the following is an example of personification?**
   - (A) The sun was like a huge orange ball.
   - (B) Jake ran as fast as a cheetah.
   - (C) The children played in the sparkling ocean water.
   - (D) The ocean waves roared onto the shore.

How Am I Doing?

Mini-Test 1

Page 19

Number Correct

4 answers correct	**Great Job!** Move on to the section test on page 59.
2–3 answers correct	**You're almost there!** But you still need a little practice. Review the practice pages 8–17 before moving on to the section test on page 59.
0–1 answer correct	**Oops!** Time to review what you have learned and try again. Review the practice section on pages 8–17. Then, retake the test on page 19. Now, move on to the section test on page 59.

Mini-Test 2

Pages 39–40

Number Correct

13–15 answers correct	**Awesome!** Move on to the section test on page 59.
10–12 answers correct	**You're almost there!** But you still need a little practice. Review the practice pages 21–38 before moving on to the section test on page 59.
0–9 answers correct	**Oops!** Time to review what you have learned and try again. Review the practice section on pages 21–38. Then, retake the test on page 39. Now, move on to the section test on page 59.

Mini-Test 3

Pages 56–57

Number Correct

8–9 answers correct	**Great Job!** Move on to the section test on page 59.
6–7 answers correct	**You're almost there!** But you still need a little practice. Review the practice pages 42–55 before moving on to the section test on page 59.
0–5 answers correct	**Oops!** Time to review what you have learned and try again. Review the practice section on pages 42–55. Then, retake the test on page 56. Now, move on to the section test on page 59.

Final Language Arts Test
for pages 8–57

DIRECTIONS: Read the passage. Then, answer the questions.

Maternal Fish Father

In the warm and temperate waters of the world live two unusual fish: the sea horse and its relative, the pipefish.

The sea horse, so-called because its head resembles a horse, is a small fish about two to eight inches long. It swims by moving the dorsal fin on its back. It is the only fish with a prehensile tail that it uses, like a monkey, to coil around and cling to seaweed.

The pipefish is named for its long snout, which looks like a thin pipe. When its body is straight, the pipefish resembles a slender snake. Its body forms an *S* shape and is propelled by its rear fins.

But it is not appearance that makes the sea horse and pipefish unique. It is their paternal roles. With both fish, the female's responsibility ends when she lays and deposits her eggs. From that point on, the male takes over and, in a manner of speaking, gives birth to the babies.

Both the male sea horse and pipefish have pouch-like organs on their undersides in which the female deposits her eggs. Here the young fish stay and are nourished for either a few days or for several weeks, depending on the species. When the baby sea horses are ready to be born, the father sea horse attaches itself to a plant and actually goes through the pangs of childbirth. As the sea horse bends back and forth, the wall of its brood pouch contracts. With each spasm, a baby fish is introduced into the world of the sea. The birth of the baby pipefish is less dramatic. The father's pouch simply opens, and the offspring swim off on their own.

1. **What is the main idea of this passage?**
   - (A) The pipefish and the sea horse fathers are unusual because of the way their offspring are born.
   - (B) Sea horses resemble horses but have tales like monkeys.
   - (C) Female pipefish and sea horses are lazy.
   - (D) Sea horses make good pets.

2. **Which statement does not describe a sea horse?**
   - (F) The sea horse's head resembles a horse.
   - (G) The sea horse's body is propelled by a rear fin.
   - (H) The sea horse uses its snout to cling to seaweed.
   - (J) The sea horse has a prehensile tail.

3. **Which statement seems to say that the role of the pipefish is less difficult than that of the seahorse?**
   - (A) The baby pipefish swim off.
   - (B) The father's pouch simply opens.
   - (C) The pipefish's body is shaped like an *S*.
   - (D) The pipefish has a long, thin snout.

DIRECTIONS: For numbers 4–6, choose the correct verb form to match each subject in the sentences.

4. **Many animals _____ in trees.**
   - (F) live
   - (G) lives
   - (H) living
   - (J) had live

5. **The animals _____ shy and afraid of the people.**
   - (A) be
   - (B) is
   - (C) are
   - (D) been

6. **Yesterday, they _____ everyone with their news.**
   - (F) shock
   - (G) shocked
   - (H) shocks
   - (J) shocking

59

Name _____   Date _____

DIRECTIONS: Read the passage. Then, answer the questions.

(1) For many years, people in the United States used streetcars to travel in cities. (2) At first, streetcars were called *horse cars* because horses pulled them. (3) Later, streetcars were powered by steam in the 1800s, people tried to use electric power, but making electricity was considered to be too expensive. (4) In 1888, a machine was invented that made electricity inexpensively. (5) In that same year, the first electric powered streetcars were put into use they quickly replaced the steam-powered streetcar. (6) With the invention of the gas engine electric streetcars were soon replaced by buses and cars. (7) By 1930, the streetcar had begun to disappear from city streets. (8) Interest in streetcars revived in the 1970s.

7. In sentence 3, <u>steam in</u> is best written —
   - (A) steam; in
   - (B) steam, in
   - (C) steam. In
   - (D) As it is

8. In sentence 5, <u>use they</u> is best written —
   - (F) use: They
   - (G) use because they
   - (H) use; they
   - (J) As it is

9. In sentence 6, <u>gas engine electric</u> is best written —
   - (A) gas, engine, electric
   - (B) gas, engine electric
   - (C) gas engine, electric
   - (D) As it is

DIRECTIONS: Read the phrases. Choose the phrase in which the underlined word is not spelled correctly.

10.
   - (F) sit on the <u>balcony</u>
   - (G) the <u>abominible</u> snowman
   - (H) <u>alkaline</u> battery
   - (J) the dog <u>yelped</u>

11.
   - (A) <u>apology</u> accepted
   - (B) filled with <u>awe</u>
   - (C) <u>dispise</u> spiders
   - (D) <u>jostled</u> in the crowd

12.
   - (F) our <u>residance</u>
   - (G) <u>adhesive</u> tape
   - (H) <u>compose</u> a sonnet
   - (J) nouns and <u>adjectives</u>

13.
   - (A) cast your <u>ballot</u>
   - (B) buy a <u>trinkette</u>
   - (C) drive the <u>vehicle</u>
   - (D) play the <u>lyre</u>

DIRECTIONS: Choose the answer that best combines the sentences.

14. **Gordon is going to the store.
    Samantha is going with him.**
   - (F) Gordon is going to the store and so is Samantha.
   - (G) Gordon and Samantha are going to the store.
   - (H) To the store, Gordon and Samantha are going.
   - (J) Gordon and Samantha to the store are going.

15. Please go to the refrigerator.
    I would like you to get a soda for me.
    - (A) Please go to the refrigerator to get me a soda.
    - (B) Please go to the refrigerator to get me a soda, because I want one.
    - (C) For me, please go to the refrigerator to get a soda.
    - (D) I would like for you to please go to the refrigerator to get a soda for me.

16. Ms. Lightfoot loves dancing.
    She goes to the dance studio every day.
    She goes at eight o'clock.
    - (F) Ms. Lightfoot loves dancing, and she goes to the dance studio every day at eight o'clock.
    - (G) Ms. Lightfoot goes to the dance studio every day at eight o'clock, because she loves dancing.
    - (H) Ms. Lightfoot loves dancing every day at the studio at eight o'clock.
    - (J) Every day, Ms. Lightfoot loves going to the dance studio to dance at eight o'clock.

17. We have a television in our family room. We enjoy watching television together as a family.
    - (A) In the family room is our television, which we enjoy together as a family.
    - (B) Our television is in the family room, which my family enjoys together.
    - (C) My family enjoys watching television together in the family room.
    - (D) My family enjoys in the family room watching television.

18. There was a very heavy rain. The police officer said we would have to take a detour.
    - (F) Because of the heavy rain, we had to take a detour the police officer said.
    - (G) The police officer said because of the heavy rain, we had to take a detour.
    - (H) The police officer told us to take a detour because of the heavy rain.
    - (J) We had to take a detour, said the police officer, in spite of the heavy rain.

DIRECTIONS: Choose the best answer.

19. Which of the following is an example of personification?
    - (A) The leaves whispered in the mild breeze.
    - (B) The loaf of bread was as hard as a rock.
    - (C) She waited as the cars zoomed by.
    - (D) The bridge was covered with ice that looked like glass.

20. Which of the following is a simile?
    - (F) The bread was not as soft as it should have been.
    - (G) The bread was left out and became stale.
    - (H) The bread was as hard as a rock.
    - (J) The bread was delicious with strawberry jam.

21. Which of the following is a metaphor?
    - (A) His harsh words were difficult for Dana to take.
    - (B) His words were hammers, pounding at Dana.
    - (C) Dana was upset by his harsh words.
    - (D) His harsh words made Dana's head pound.

GO

DIRECTIONS: Read the following passage. Then, answer the questions.

One afternoon in March, I found two silver dollars shining in a half-melted snow bank. I instantly thought of buried treasure. So, I dug through the snow searching for more. All I ended up with were two really cold hands. I slipped the two coins in my pocket and went home colder but richer.

The next morning, Megan and her little sister were searching the snow banks. *Finders keepers* was my first thought. I didn't need to get to the losers weepers part since Moira was already crying for real. "I dropped them right here," she said between tears. Her hands were red from digging in the snow. "Maybe they got shoved down the street by the snow plow. Let's try over there," Megan said optimistically.

They'll never know was my second thought, as I walked past them toward Tyler's house.

"Phil, have you seen two silver dollars?" Megan called. Moira looked up from the snow bank with hope bright in her eyes.

"Coins?" *Look innocent* was my third thought.

"Yes, Moira dropped two silver dollars somewhere around here yesterday."

"Yeah," said Moira, "they're big and heavy." She brushed her icy red hands off on her jacket and wiped the tears from her eyes. Her eyes were as red as her hands.

I hesitated, but only for a moment. Then, I said, "As a matter of fact, I dug two coins out of that snow bank yesterday. I wondered who might have lost them." Moira ran to me and gave me a bear hug. "Oh, thank you, thank you!" I couldn't help but smile.

22. **What is the theme of this story?**
    - (F) It is okay to lie if you think you will get away with it.
    - (G) It is always better to be honest than rich.
    - (H) "Finders keepers, losers weepers" is not a good saying to live by.
    - (J) Both G and H apply.

23. **What is the setting of this story?**
    - (A) outside on a March day
    - (B) outside on a warm, sunny day
    - (C) inside on a rainy spring day
    - (D) the view outside a window

24. **Overall, what type of person is Phil?**
    - (F) ambitious and unfair
    - (G) honest and caring
    - (H) greedy and cruel
    - (J) dishonest and angry

25. **How did Phil probably feel at the end of the story? He felt _____.**
    - (A) angry with himself for being honest
    - (B) angry with Megan and Moira
    - (C) hopeful that he would find another buried treasure
    - (D) disappointed at having to give up the coins but glad that he had been honest

Name _____ Date _____

Final Language Arts Test
Answer Sheet

1. Ⓐ Ⓑ Ⓒ Ⓓ
2. Ⓕ Ⓖ Ⓗ Ⓙ
3. Ⓐ Ⓑ Ⓒ Ⓓ
4. Ⓕ Ⓖ Ⓗ Ⓙ
5. Ⓐ Ⓑ Ⓒ Ⓓ
6. Ⓕ Ⓖ Ⓗ Ⓙ
7. Ⓐ Ⓑ Ⓒ Ⓓ
8. Ⓕ Ⓖ Ⓗ Ⓙ
9. Ⓐ Ⓑ Ⓒ Ⓓ
10. Ⓕ Ⓖ Ⓗ Ⓙ

11. Ⓐ Ⓑ Ⓒ Ⓓ
12. Ⓕ Ⓖ Ⓗ Ⓙ
13. Ⓐ Ⓑ Ⓒ Ⓓ
14. Ⓕ Ⓖ Ⓗ Ⓙ
15. Ⓐ Ⓑ Ⓒ Ⓓ
16. Ⓕ Ⓖ Ⓗ Ⓙ
17. Ⓐ Ⓑ Ⓒ Ⓓ
18. Ⓕ Ⓖ Ⓗ Ⓙ
19. Ⓐ Ⓑ Ⓒ Ⓓ
20. Ⓕ Ⓖ Ⓗ Ⓙ

21. Ⓐ Ⓑ Ⓒ Ⓓ
22. Ⓕ Ⓖ Ⓗ Ⓙ
23. Ⓐ Ⓑ Ⓒ Ⓓ
24. Ⓕ Ⓖ Ⓗ Ⓙ
25. Ⓐ Ⓑ Ⓒ Ⓓ

New York Mathematics Content Standards

New York City Standards

The mathematics section of the New York City Standards measures knowledge in five different areas.

1. Arithmetic and Number Concepts
2. Geometry and Measurement Concepts
3. Function and Algebra Concepts
4. Statistics and Probability Concepts
5. Mathematical Process

New York State Standards

The mathematics section of the New York State Standards measures knowledge in two different areas:

1. Analysis, Inquiry, and Design
    - *1.1:* Mathematical Analysis
3. Mathematics
    - *3.1:* Mathematical Reasoning
    - *3.2:* Number and Numeration
    - *3.3:* Operations
    - *3.4:* Modeling/Multiple Representation
    - *3.5:* Measurement
    - *3.6:* Uncertainty
    - *3.7:* Patterns/Functions

New York Mathematics Table of Contents

Arithmetic and Number Concepts
- Standards and What They Mean 65
- Practice Pages 66
- Mini-Test 1 91

Geometry and Measurement Concepts
- Standards and What They Mean 93
- Practice Pages 94
- Mini-Test 2 114

Function and Algebra Concepts
- Standards and What They Mean 116
- Practice Pages 117
- Mini-Test 3 131

Statistics and Probability Concepts
- Standards and What They Mean 132
- Practice Pages 133
- Mini-Test 4 147

Mathematical Process
- Standards and What They Mean 148
- Practice Pages 149
- Mini-Test 5 154

How Am I Doing? 155

Final Mathematics Test 157
- Answer Sheet 163

Mathematics Standards

1.0 Arithmetic and Number Concepts
By the end of the school year, students should:

1.A Continue to use place value and expanded notation to read and write numbers to one billion and decimal numbers through the thousandths place. *(See pages 66–67.)*

1.B Reinforce place value by using powers of ten (exponential notation). *(See page 68.)*

1.C Explore the concept of scientific notation. *(See page 68.)*

1.D Estimate whole numbers by rounding through ten thousand and decimals to the nearest hundredths. *(See page 69.)*

1.E Round fractional and decimal numbers for estimates in computation. *(See page 70.)*

1.F Use estimation to check the reasonableness of results. *(See page 71.)*

1.G Understand and use special numbers, such as primes, composite numbers, square numbers, common divisors, and common multiples. *(See pages 72–74.)*

> **What it means:**
> - **Prime numbers** are whole numbers that have only two factors, 1 and itself. Examples of prime numbers are 1, 3, 11, 13, and 17.
> - A **composite number** is a whole number that has more than two factors. For example, 12 is a composite number because 1, 2, 3, 4, 6, and 12 are its factors.
> - A **multiple** is the result of a number multiplied by any whole number. For example, the multiples of 5 are 0, 5, 10, 15, 20, and so on.

1.H Continue to add, subtract, multiply, and divide whole numbers and extend division to the use of three-digit divisors. *(See page 75.)*

1.I Add, subtract, multiply, and divide fractions and mixed numbers with and without common denominators and express fractions in simplest form. *(See pages 76–78.)*

1.J Use equivalent forms of fractions, decimals, and percents. *(See page 79.)*

1.K Compare common fractions and decimals. *(See page 80.)*

1.L Add, subtract, multiply, and divide decimals. *(See page 81.)*

1.M Find a percent of a number. *(See page 82.)*

1.N Use the number line to model a variety of numbers. *(See page 83.)*

1.O Relate positive and negative numbers to real-life situations (e.g., loss and gain in bank transactions). *(See page 84.)*

1.P Explore addition and subtraction of integers using the number line. *(See page 85.)*

1.Q Explore negative number notation to fractions on the number line. *(See page 86.)*

1.R Understand and apply the order of operations. *(See page 87.)*

1.S Express a fraction as a ratio. *(See page 88.)*

1.T Identify equal ratios as proportions. *(See page 89.)*

1.U Use ratio and proportion concepts to solve problems. *(See page 90.)*

Name _____ Date _____

Mathematics

 1.A

Place Value

Arithmetic and Number Concepts

DIRECTIONS: Write the correct numeral for each number.

1. Five hundred sixty-two thousand, one hundred seventy-four
   _____

2. Two hundred million, five hundred eighteen thousand, seven hundred thirty-six _____

3. Sixty-five billion, two hundred seventy million, nine hundred forty-eight thousand, three hundred one _____

DIRECTIONS: Match the underlined digit with its place value.

4. ____ 5.71<u>2</u>3   a. two hundreds

5. ____ <u>2</u>08.0023   b. two thousandths

6. ____ 0.0045<u>2</u>   c. two hundred thousandths

7. ____ 0.000<u>2</u>   d. two hundredths

8. ____ 1,230.0<u>2</u>3   e. two hundred thousands

9. ____ <u>2</u>65,300.023   f. two ten thousandths

DIRECTIONS: Rearrange the group of numbers from smallest to largest.

10. 712.01,   711.9,   712.10,   712.09,   711.95,   712.001,   711.009

Name _____ Date _____

Mathematics 1.A

Expanded Notation

Arithmetic and Number Concepts

DIRECTIONS: The following numbers are written in expanded form. Write each number in standard form.

1. $100{,}000 + 2{,}000 + 300 + 70 + 5 + \frac{3}{10} + \frac{4}{100}$ _____

2. $20{,}000 + 5{,}000 + 40 + 3 + \frac{2}{10}$ _____

3. $700{,}000 + 80{,}000 + 2{,}000 + 400 + 60 + \frac{2}{10{,}000}$ _____

4. $200{,}000{,}000 + 100{,}000 + 4{,}000 + 30 + 1 + \frac{4}{100{,}000}$ _____

5. $9{,}000{,}000 + 600{,}000 + 50{,}000 + 300$ _____

DIRECTIONS: Write each whole number in expanded form.

6. 1,200,341 _____

7. 10,650.003 _____

8. 238,200.05 _____

9. 563.00201 _____

10. 4,070,004 _____

DIRECTIONS: Write each number in word form.

11. 23,042,368 _____

12. 418,723,006 _____

13. 2,078.03 _____

14. 30,012.0005 _____

STOP

67

Exponential and Scientific Notation

Mathematics 1.B/1.C

Arithmetic and Number Concepts

DIRECTIONS: Multiples of 10 have special meaning in our number system. Find the value of the exponential expressions below.

1. $10^1 =$
2. $10^2 =$
3. $10^3 =$
4. $10^4 =$
5. $10^5 =$
6. $10^6 =$

7. What is the relationship between the value of the exponent and the number of zeros in your answer?

_____

_____

_____

DIRECTIONS: Find the decimal value for each of the following exponential expressions.

Example:

Multiplying or dividing by multiples of 10 moves the decimal point in a number. Mathematicians and scientists use exponents as shorthand for writing these operations. Multiplying means moving the decimal to the right. The 4 in the exponent tells us to move the decimal 4 places.

8.32×10^4
$8.32 \times 10^4 = 8.32 \times 10,000$

$8.32 \smile\smile\smile\smile = 83,200$

8. $2.4569 \times 10^3 =$
9. $5.9 \times 10^2 =$
10. $6.15892 \times 10^5 =$

11. $2.34 \times 10^1 =$
12. $6.8 \times 10^4 =$
13. $5.3498 \times 10^6 =$

14. $76.4 \times 10^2 =$
15. $18.39426 \times 10^5 =$
16. $73.215 \times 10^3 =$

Name _____ Date _____

Mathematics

1.D

Rounding Numbers

Arithmetic and Number Concepts

DIRECTIONS: Choose the answer that rounds the number to the correct place indicated.

1. Which of the following shows 28,123 rounded to the nearest ten thousand?
   - (A) 30,000
   - (B) 29,000
   - (C) 28,000
   - (D) 39,000

2. Which of the following shows 43,666 rounded to the nearest thousand?
   - (F) 43,000
   - (G) 44,000
   - (H) 43,700
   - (J) 43,670

3. Which of the following shows 92,232 rounded to the nearest ten thousand?
   - (A) 91,000
   - (B) 93,000
   - (C) 92,000
   - (D) 90,000

4. Which of the following shows 49,765 rounded to the nearest hundred?
   - (F) 49,000
   - (G) 50,000
   - (H) 49,800
   - (J) 49,700

5. Which of the following shows 32.546 rounded to the nearest hundredths?
   - (A) 30.00
   - (B) 32.50
   - (C) 32.55
   - (D) 32.54

6. Which of the following shows 27.81 rounded to the nearest tenths?
   - (F) 27.8
   - (G) 27.9
   - (H) 28.0
   - (J) 30.0

7. Which of the following shows 74.668 rounded to the nearest hundredths?
   - (A) 74.65
   - (B) 74.0
   - (C) 74.7
   - (D) 74.67

8. Which of the following shows 92.232 rounded to the nearest hundredths?
   - (F) 90.00
   - (G) 92.23
   - (H) 92.20
   - (J) 92.00

STOP

Name _____ Date _____

Mathematics
1.E

Rounding Decimals and Fractions

Arithmetic and Number Concepts

DIRECTIONS: Use estimation to answer the following questions. Round the values to a whole number and then do the arithmetic in your head. Write your answers in complete sentences. Include number sentences to show how you came up with your answer.

1. Anita works part-time at a fast-food restaurant where she makes $8.35 an hour. The first week she worked 13.5 hours. Approximately $10 will come out of her paycheck for taxes. Will she have enough money to buy a CD player costing $104.94?

   _____
   _____
   _____
   _____

2. The school's carnival committee is working late. They decide to order pizza. There are 24 students and one teacher on the committee. There are 18 slices in a large pizza. How many large pizzas should they buy to make sure each person gets at least two slices? If a large pizza costs $16.67, about how much will each person need to chip in?

   _____
   _____
   _____
   _____

3. Mr. Silverman is tiling his rectangular kitchen floor. The dimensions of the floor are $12\frac{2}{3}$ ft. by $10\frac{1}{8}$ ft. The tile he wants costs $1.80 per square foot. About how much will he have to pay for tile?

   _____
   _____
   _____
   _____

4. A small company is pricing out computer systems. A basic system costs $5,718. A larger system, which will allow for growth, costs $38,249. About how much more will the larger system cost?

   _____
   _____
   _____

5. Jorgé has three $50 bills to shop for school clothes. He selects a new pair of sneakers for $36, four shirts costing $11.50 each, and two pairs of jeans costing $21.99 each. Will he have enough money to cover the purchases?

   _____
   _____
   _____
   _____

70

Mathematics
1.F

Using Estimation to Check Answers

Arithmetic and Number Concepts

DIRECTIONS: Here are some arithmetic problems other students performed. Some of the answers may be incorrect. Use estimation to quickly identify which answers are wrong. Next to each wrong answer, write your best estimate of the correct answer. Then, check your work by calculating the exact answers.

Examples:

Estimating: Round the numbers so they are easier to work with. Then, mentally perform the operation to get an approximate solution.

$$365 \times 42$$
$$\approx 370 \times 40$$
$$\approx 14{,}800$$

$$4{,}773 + 2{,}531$$
$$\approx 5{,}000 + 2{,}500$$
$$\approx 7{,}500$$

$$72{,}340 \div 3{,}291$$
$$\approx 72{,}000 \div 3{,}000$$
$$\approx 24$$

1.
```
   735
 ×  29
 2,131
```

2.
```
  45,705
− 23,369
  22,336
```

3.
```
       218 R10
 35)76,412
```

4.
```
   2,413
 ×   620
 149,606
```

5.
```
 1,273,412
 +  99,655
 2,373,067
```

6.
```
         21
 312)6,552
```

7.
```
     473
 ×   684
 1,323,532
```

8.
```
    390
 +7,930
  9,320
```

71

Name _____ Date _____

Mathematics
1.G   # Prime and Composite Numbers

Arithmetic and Number Concepts

DIRECTIONS: Fill in the factor trees by multiplying. The numbers in the first row are the prime factors of the composite number at the root of the tree.

1.
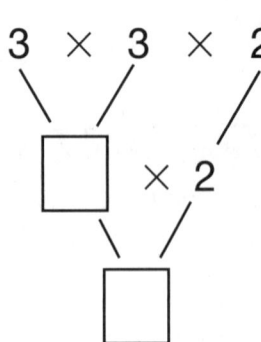

2.
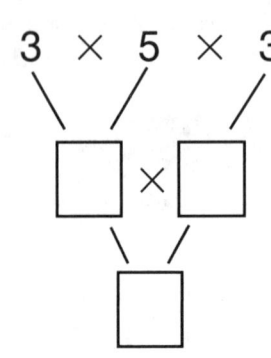

3.
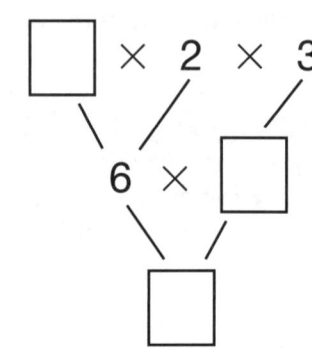

4.
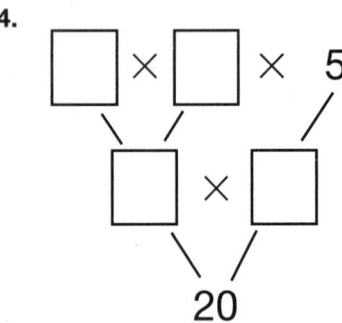

5.
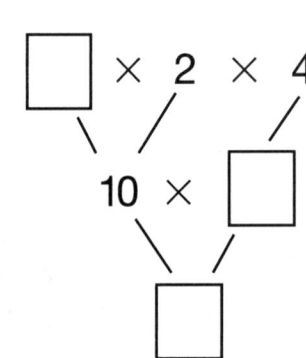

6.
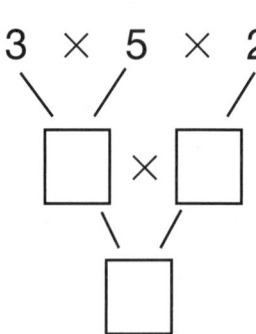

7.
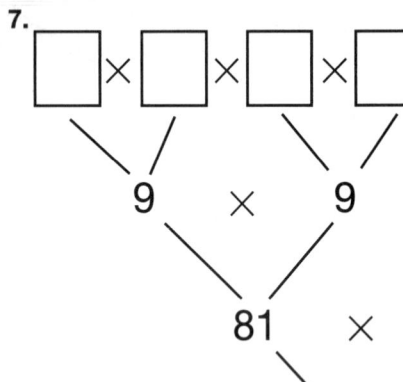

8.
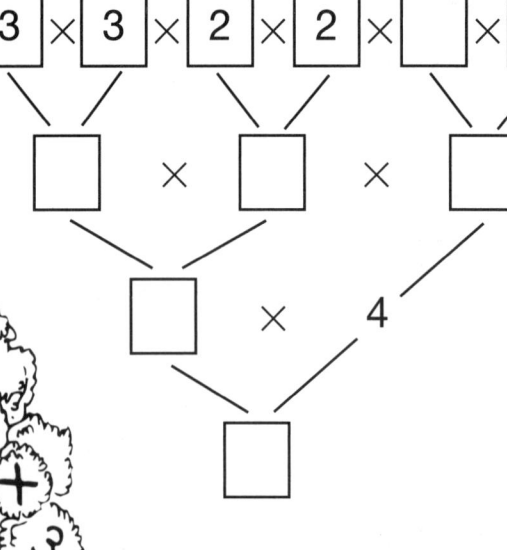

72

Name _____   Date _____

Mathematics
1.G

Square Numbers

Arithmetic and Number Concepts

DIRECTIONS: Find the square root for numbers 1–6.

DIRECTIONS: Find the square for numbers 7–12.

1. $\sqrt{25}$
   - (A) 7
   - (B) 5
   - (C) 4
   - (D) 6

2. $\sqrt{81}$
   - (F) 11
   - (G) 7
   - (H) 8
   - (J) 9

3. $\sqrt{144}$
   - (A) 11
   - (B) 12
   - (C) 13
   - (D) 14

4. $\sqrt{256}$
   - (F) 16
   - (G) 25
   - (H) 15
   - (J) 21

5. $\sqrt{64}$
   - (A) 7
   - (B) 5
   - (C) 8
   - (D) 6

6. $\sqrt{36}$
   - (F) 5
   - (G) 6
   - (H) 8
   - (J) 9

7. $4^2 = $ _____
   - (A) 8
   - (B) 12
   - (C) 16
   - (D) 20

8. $11^2 = $ _____
   - (F) 111
   - (G) 121
   - (H) 144
   - (J) 110

9. $15^2 = $ _____
   - (A) 300
   - (B) 250
   - (C) 150
   - (D) 225

10. $7^2 = $ _____
    - (F) 28
    - (G) 42
    - (H) 49
    - (J) 64

11. $20^2 = $ _____
    - (A) 200
    - (B) 250
    - (C) 400
    - (D) 4,000

12. $8^2 = $ _____
    - (F) 56
    - (G) 72
    - (H) 16
    - (J) 64

STOP

Mathematics
1.G

Least Common Multiples and Greatest Common Divisors

Arithmetic and Number Concepts

DIRECTIONS: Use the table for the example and questions 1–5. Find the least common multiple and greatest common divisor as necessary to add and subtract the fractions.

Today's Workouts	
Kerri	$1\frac{1}{2}$ hours
Jennifer	$\frac{3}{4}$ hour
Ahmad	2 hours
Risa	$\frac{2}{3}$ hour

1. Who had a longer workout, Jennifer or Risa? How much longer?

    Ⓐ Jennifer, $\frac{1}{12}$ hour

    Ⓑ Jennifer, $\frac{1}{2}$ hour

    Ⓒ Risa, $\frac{1}{12}$ hour

    Ⓓ Risa, $\frac{1}{2}$ hour

2. How much longer was Ahmad's workout than Kerri's workout?

    Ⓕ 1 hour

    Ⓖ 2 hours

    Ⓗ $3\frac{1}{2}$ hours

    Ⓙ $\frac{1}{2}$ hour

3. Risa finished her workout just as Kerri started hers. How long did it take from the time Risa started until Kerri finished?

    Ⓐ $1\frac{3}{5}$ hours

    Ⓑ $2\frac{1}{6}$ hours

    Ⓒ $\frac{5}{6}$ hour

    Ⓓ $1\frac{5}{6}$ hours

4. Kerri and Jennifer started their workouts at the same time. Who finished first and by how much?

    Ⓕ Kerri, $2\frac{1}{4}$ hours

    Ⓖ Kerri, $\frac{3}{4}$ hour

    Ⓗ Jennifer, $2\frac{1}{4}$ hours

    Ⓙ Jennifer, $\frac{3}{4}$ hour

5. What was the total workout time for all four people on the list?

    Ⓐ 4 hours

    Ⓑ $4\frac{11}{12}$ hours

    Ⓒ $3\frac{6}{9}$ hours

    Ⓓ $4\frac{6}{9}$ hours

STOP

Name _____ Date _____

Mathematics
1.H

Whole Numbers (All Operations)

Arithmetic and Number Concepts

DIRECTIONS: Read and work each problem. Be sure that you are performing the correct operation. Fill in the circle for your choice.

Clue: If the answer you find is not one of the answer choices, rework the problem on scratch paper. If you rework a problem and still find that the right number is not given, mark the choice for "None of the above."

1. 678
   1,234
   + 679
   - Ⓐ 2,491
   - Ⓑ 1,591
   - Ⓒ 2,591
   - Ⓓ None of the above

2. 6,789 ÷ 144 =
   - Ⓕ 47R12
   - Ⓖ 47R21
   - Ⓗ 47R16
   - Ⓙ None of the above

3. 756 × 432 =
   - Ⓐ 236,592
   - Ⓑ 326,592
   - Ⓒ 336,592
   - Ⓓ None of the above

4. 123,489
   − 79,654
   - Ⓕ 42,835
   - Ⓖ 93,143
   - Ⓗ 43,834
   - Ⓙ None of the above

5. 4,988
   + 8,765
   - Ⓐ 12,753
   - Ⓑ 13,853
   - Ⓒ 13,753
   - Ⓓ None of the above

6. 456 + 768 + 654 =
   - Ⓕ 1,878
   - Ⓖ 2,468
   - Ⓗ 1,468
   - Ⓙ None of the above

7. 45,676
   + 78,543
   - Ⓐ 124,219
   - Ⓑ 115,219
   - Ⓒ 134,129
   - Ⓓ None of the above

8. 248)7,945
   - Ⓕ 32R4
   - Ⓖ 22R9
   - Ⓗ 32R9
   - Ⓙ None of the above

9. 812 × 789 =
   - Ⓐ 1,640,668
   - Ⓑ 560,668
   - Ⓒ 640,668
   - Ⓓ None of the above

10. 45,678
    123,602
    + 345,999
    - Ⓕ 525,279
    - Ⓖ 815,279
    - Ⓗ 515,278
    - Ⓙ None of the above

STOP

Name _____ Date _____

Mathematics
1.1

Adding and Subtracting Fractions

Arithmetic and Number Concepts

DIRECTIONS: Fill in the circle for the correct answer to each addition and subtraction problem. Choose "None of the above" if the right answer is not given.

1. $\frac{5}{6} + \frac{1}{12} + \frac{1}{3} =$
   - Ⓐ $\frac{7}{3}$
   - Ⓑ $1\frac{1}{4}$
   - Ⓒ $\frac{11}{12}$
   - Ⓓ None of the above

2. $20\frac{2}{5} + 5\frac{5}{6} =$
   - Ⓕ $26\frac{7}{30}$
   - Ⓖ $25\frac{7}{12}$
   - Ⓗ $36\frac{3}{10}$
   - Ⓙ None of the above

3. $4\frac{2}{10}$
   $-\ 3\frac{4}{5}$
   - Ⓐ $1\frac{4}{10}$
   - Ⓑ $\frac{2}{5}$
   - Ⓒ $\frac{2}{8}$
   - Ⓓ None of the above

4. $12\frac{2}{3} - 9\frac{5}{6} =$
   - Ⓕ $2\frac{2}{3}$
   - Ⓖ $22\frac{1}{2}$
   - Ⓗ $2\frac{5}{6}$
   - Ⓙ None of the above

5. $\frac{7}{10} + \frac{8}{10} =$
   - Ⓐ $1\frac{7}{10}$
   - Ⓑ $\frac{10}{18}$
   - Ⓒ $1\frac{4}{5}$
   - Ⓓ None of the above

6. $\frac{8}{10}$
   $-\ \frac{5}{10}$
   - Ⓕ $1\frac{3}{10}$
   - Ⓖ $\frac{3}{10}$
   - Ⓗ $\frac{1}{5}$
   - Ⓙ None of the above

7. $18\frac{3}{4}$
   $+\ 13\frac{5}{8}$
   - Ⓐ $33\frac{5}{8}$
   - Ⓑ $5\frac{1}{8}$
   - Ⓒ $32\frac{3}{8}$
   - Ⓓ None of the above

8. $8\frac{1}{3} - 6\frac{5}{6} =$
   - Ⓕ $1\frac{1}{3}$
   - Ⓖ $2\frac{1}{6}$
   - Ⓗ $15\frac{1}{6}$
   - Ⓙ None of the above

9. $1\frac{4}{5} + 6\frac{2}{3} =$
   - Ⓐ $7\frac{1}{3}$
   - Ⓑ $8\frac{2}{15}$
   - Ⓒ $8\frac{7}{15}$
   - Ⓓ None of the above

10. $12\frac{1}{2}$
    $-\ 7\frac{3}{4}$
    - Ⓕ $3\frac{3}{4}$
    - Ⓖ $4\frac{3}{4}$
    - Ⓗ $20\frac{1}{4}$
    - Ⓙ None of the above

76

Mathematics

1.1

Multiplying Fractions and Mixed Numbers

Arithmetic and Number Concepts

DIRECTIONS: Complete these tables.

Table 1

✕	$\frac{3}{5}$	$\frac{1}{2}$	$\frac{2}{3}$	$\frac{1}{6}$	$\frac{1}{8}$
$\frac{1}{2}$	$\frac{3}{10}$				
$\frac{3}{8}$					
$\frac{4}{7}$					
$\frac{5}{8}$					
$\frac{1}{10}$					

Table 2

✕	$\frac{1}{2}$	$\frac{3}{4}$	$\frac{1}{6}$	$\frac{3}{8}$	$\frac{1}{3}$
$\frac{1}{4}$					
$\frac{1}{8}$					
$\frac{1}{5}$					
$\frac{2}{7}$					
$\frac{1}{3}$					

DIRECTIONS: Multiply and reduce the mixed numbers to their lowest terms.

1. $2\frac{2}{3} \times 3\frac{1}{4} =$

2. $3\frac{7}{9} \times 1\frac{7}{8} =$

3. $4\frac{2}{8} \times 5\frac{3}{5} =$

4. $4\frac{1}{3} \times 7\frac{1}{2} =$

5. $5\frac{3}{8} \times 4\frac{3}{4} =$

6. $\frac{6}{7} \times 5\frac{2}{8} =$

STOP

Mathematics 1.1 — Dividing Fractions

Arithmetic and Number Concepts

DIRECTIONS: Divide. Write answers in lowest terms.

1. $\dfrac{4}{5} \div \dfrac{2}{5} =$

2. $1\dfrac{1}{2} \div 18 =$

3. $0 \div \dfrac{2}{3} =$

4. $1 \div 7\dfrac{1}{2} =$

5. $\dfrac{9}{10} \div \dfrac{1}{5} =$

6. $4\dfrac{2}{5} \div \dfrac{1}{4} =$

7. $4\dfrac{1}{2} \div 18 =$

8. $\dfrac{5}{14} \div \dfrac{1}{2} =$

9. $4\dfrac{1}{3} \div \dfrac{26}{27} =$

10. $\dfrac{9}{10} \div \dfrac{9}{10} =$

11. $3\dfrac{5}{8} \div 8 =$

12. $3\dfrac{2}{5} \div \dfrac{2}{3} =$

13. $6 \div 1\dfrac{1}{2} =$

14. $3\dfrac{5}{8} \div 1\dfrac{5}{24} =$

15. $\dfrac{12}{21} \div 7\dfrac{1}{3} =$

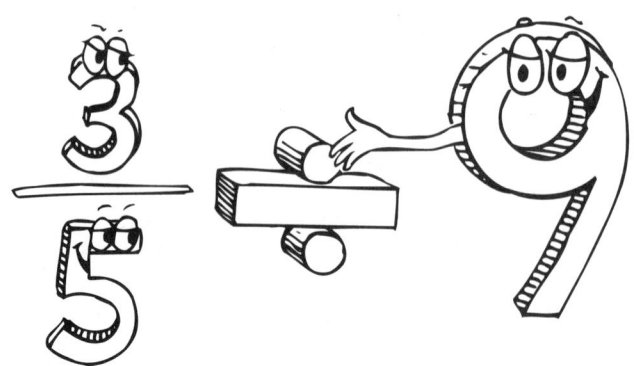

Name _____ Date _____

Mathematics
1.J

Percents, Decimals, and Fractions

Arithmetic and Number Concepts

Examples:

Fraction to Decimal:
The fraction bar means divide.

$\frac{3}{5} = 3 \div 5$ $5\overline{)3.0}$ ($.6$, $\underline{30}$, 0) $\frac{3}{5} = 0.6$

Decimal to Percent:
Move the decimal two places to the right.

$0.08 = 8\%$
$0.73 = 73\%$

Percent to Decimal:
Move the decimal two places to the left.

$42\% = 0.42$
$1.87\% = 0.0187$

Decimal to Fraction:
Write the digits over the appropriate place value and reduce to lowest terms.

$0.35 = $ thirty-five hundredths $= \frac{35}{100} = \frac{7}{20}$

$0.015 = $ fifteen thousandths $= \frac{15}{1000} = \frac{3}{200}$

Percent (%) means *per hundred*. It is a ratio that compares a number to 100. It is the number of hundredths.

DIRECTIONS: Write each fraction in decimal form.

1. $\frac{4}{5}$ _____   2. $\frac{3}{8}$ _____   3. $\frac{5}{3}$ _____   4. $\frac{7}{9}$ _____

DIRECTIONS: Change each percent to its decimal form.

5. 39% _____   6. 7% _____   7. 1.8% _____   8. 132% _____   9. 0.05% _____

DIRECTIONS: Change each decimal to its percent form.

10. 0.87 _____   11. 1.20 _____   12. 0.45 _____   13. 0.02 _____   14. 0.342 _____

DIRECTIONS: Change each decimal to a fraction.

15. 0.6 _____   16. 0.42 _____   17. 0.025 _____   18. 0.85 _____   19. 1.92 _____

STOP

79

Name _____ Date _____

Mathematics 1.K

Fractions to Decimals

Arithmetic and Number Concepts

DIRECTIONS: Write each fraction as a decimal.

1. $\dfrac{7}{10}$ = _____

2. $\dfrac{78}{100}$ = _____

3. $\dfrac{3}{4}$ = _____

4. $\dfrac{2}{10}$ = _____

5. $\dfrac{2}{3}$ = _____

6. $\dfrac{5}{8}$ = _____

7. $\dfrac{4}{100}$ = _____

8. $8\dfrac{103}{1000}$ = _____

9. $\dfrac{3}{10}$ = _____

10. $\dfrac{21}{1000}$ = _____

11. $\dfrac{3}{5}$ = _____

12. $\dfrac{1}{2}$ = _____

13. $5\dfrac{4}{100}$ = _____

14. $1\dfrac{8}{10}$ = _____

15. $14\dfrac{7}{100}$ = _____

16. $\dfrac{6}{10}$ = _____

17. $\dfrac{31}{100}$ = _____

18. $5\dfrac{24}{1000}$ = _____

19. $7\dfrac{6}{10}$ = _____

20. $15\dfrac{6}{10}$ = _____

21. $\dfrac{1}{4}$ = _____

STOP

Name _____ Date _____

Mathematics
1.L

Decimal Operations

Arithmetic and Number Concepts

DIRECTIONS: Work each problem. Shade in the correct answers to find the frog's path to the bug.

1. 0.43
    0.06
    0.28
    0.77
    + 1.01

2. 35.1
    475.11
    0.54
    0.3
    + 1.5

3. 377.5
    × 1.53

4. 0.35)2.9365

5. 0.4392
    × 0.216

6. 5.03
    0.371
    0.51
    1.22
    + 1.3

7. 0.8627
    × 0.456

8. 5.621
    × 4.87

9. 10.3500
    − 2.3844

10. 5.764
    + 0.49

11. 8.879
    − 2.933

12. 83.9)387.0307

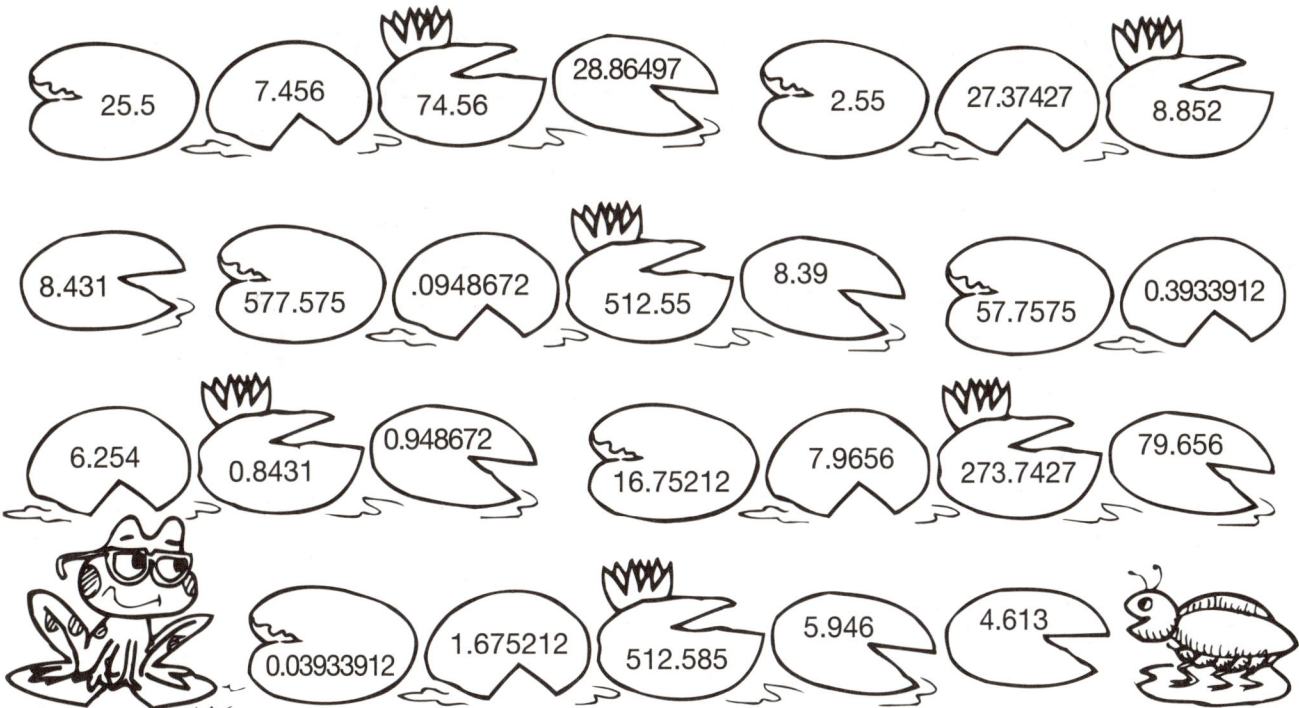

81

Name _____ Date _____

Mathematics

1.M

Finding the Percent of a Number

Arithmetic and Number Concepts

DIRECTIONS: Find the answers to the following questions and put the corresponding letter above each answer.

 Only one of the Seven Wonders of the Ancient World still exists. Which one is it?

A. How much is 4% of 20?

P. 90% of 56 is how much?

D. How much is 125% of 4?

R. 0.3% of 880 is how much?

F. How much is 72% of 6?

T. 15% of 80 is how much?

E. How much is 220% of 665?

S. 130% of 7 is how much?

O. How much is 5% of 17?

M. 38% of 45 is how much?

Y. How much is 70% of 15?

Y. 2% of 90 is how much?

I. How much is 1.5% of 900?

G. 150% of 6 is how much?

P. How much is 0.85% of 1,000?

| 8.5 | 10.5 | 2.64 | 0.8 | 17.1 | 13.5 | 5 | 9.1 |

| 0.85 | 4.32 | 1,463 | 9 | 1.8 | 50.4 | 12 |

82

Name _____ Date _____

Mathematics
1.N

Using a Number Line

Arithmetic and Number Concepts

DIRECTIONS: Fill in the empty spaces on the number line below. Use the values in the number bank.

1.

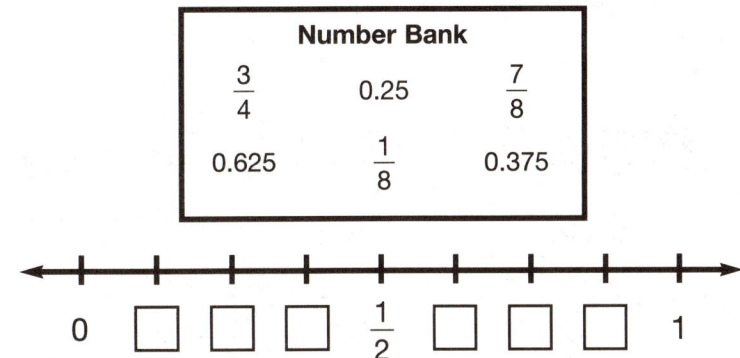

DIRECTIONS: Match each fraction in numbers 2–10 with the letter representing its spot on the number line. Write the letter next to the problem.

_____ 2. $\frac{10}{11}$

_____ 3. $\frac{5}{9}$

_____ 4. $\frac{1}{6}$

_____ 5. $\frac{3}{5}$

_____ 6. $\frac{1}{3}$

_____ 7. $\frac{3}{4}$

_____ 8. $\frac{7}{8}$

_____ 9. $\frac{1}{16}$

_____ 10. $\frac{4}{16}$

STOP

Name _____ Date _____

Mathematics

1.0

Managing a Checking Account

Arithmetic and Number Concepts

DIRECTIONS: The spreadsheet below shows transactions from a checking account. A withdrawal occurs when you take money out of the account. A deposit represents money that is put into the account. The balance is the amount of money in the account at that point.

For the 9 transactions shown below, write a number sentence showing how to get the balance. Then, write the balance in the spreadsheet. The first transaction has been done for you.

Trans. #	Date	Item	Withdrawal	Deposit	Balance
	10/1				$1,378.98
1	10/1	Rent	$1,050.00		$ 328.98
2	10/3	Groceries	$223.42		
3	10/3	Cash	$40.00		
4	10/5	Phone Bill	$36.30		
5	10/7	Paycheck		$523.81	
6	10/7	Car Payment	$178.46		
7	10/8	Birthday		$30.00	
8	10/10	Electric Bill	$48.23		
9	10/12	Car Insurance	$298.60		
10					
11					
12					

1. $1,378.98 − $1,050.00 = $328.98

2.

3.

4.

5.

6.

7.

8.

9.

DIRECTIONS: Fill in the remainder of the spreadsheet for each transaction listed below.

10. A friend pays back a loan of $40 on October 14.

11. Buy something on October 16 that will not cause an overdraft (a negative value).

12. You receive another paycheck on October 22.

Adding and Subtracting Integers on a Number Line

DIRECTIONS: Use the number line below to answer the questions.

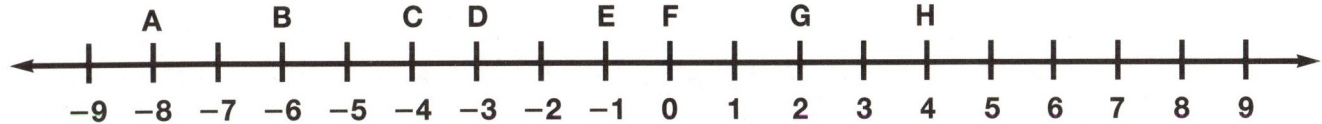

1. What letter on the number line shows the answer to the following: −6 + −2? _____

2. What letter on the number line shows the answer to the following: 7 + −5? _____

3. What letter on the number line shows the answer to the following: −9 + 9? _____

4. What letter on the number line shows the answer to the following: 2 − 5? _____

5. What letter on the number line shows the answer to the following: 0 − 4? _____

6. What letter on the number line shows the answer to the following: −2 + −4? _____

7. What letter on the number line shows the answer to the following: 4 + −5? _____

8. What letter on the number line shows the answer to the following: −5 + 9? _____

9. Write the letter I above the corresponding number on the number line that shows the answer to the following: −7 + 16.

_____

Name _____ Date _____

Mathematics

1.Q

Adding and Subtracting Negative Fractions on a Number Line

Arithmetic and Number Concepts

DIRECTIONS: Use the number line below to answer the questions.

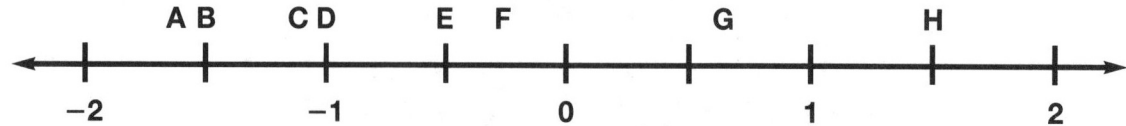

1. What letter on the number line indicates $-\frac{1}{2}$?
   _____

2. What letter on the number line shows the answer to the following: $+2 - +1\frac{3}{8}$?
   _____

3. What letter on the number line shows the answer to the following: $-\frac{1}{2} + -\frac{1}{2}$?
   _____

4. What letter on the number line shows the answer to the following: $+\frac{1}{2}$ and $-\frac{3}{4}$?
   _____

5. What letter on the number line shows the answer to the following: $-1\frac{5}{8} - -\frac{1}{2}$?
   _____

6. What letter on the number line indicates $-1\frac{5}{8}$? _____

7. What letter on the number line shows the answer to the following: $-1 + 2\frac{1}{2}$?
   _____

8. Write the letter I above the corresponding number on the number line that shows the answer to the following: $-\frac{3}{4} + -\frac{1}{2}$.
   _____

STOP

86

Order of Operations

Mathematics 1.R — Arithmetic and Number Concepts

DIRECTIONS: The order in which you do mathematical operations may change your answer. Mathematicians have agreed on a standard order of operations. The following phrase may help you remember the order. Each letter in the phrase stands for a mathematical operation.

Please	**P**arentheses
Excuse	**E**xponents
My	**M**ultiplication
Dear	**D**ivision
Aunt	**A**ddition
Sally	**S**ubtraction

DIRECTIONS: Follow the order of operations to find the solutions. Show your work.

1. $27 + 60 - (8 \times 12 - 48 \div 4) \div 3$

2. $-6 + 8 \times [-3(4 \times 7) + 58] + 30$

3. $\frac{1}{8}(16 - 10)$

4. $25 - [36 \div (12 + 6)] \times 8$

5. $15 - 6 \times 3 + 12 \div 3 \times 2$

6. $3^2 \times 3 + (29 - 8 \times 3)$

7. $[6(30 \div 2)] \div \frac{5}{15} - 9 \times 20$

8. $6 + 8(9 + 102 \div 17)$

9. $14 - 6 \times 2 + 20 + 4 \times 4$

10. $2^3 - 6 + [29 - 2 \times 3(1 + 4)]$

Name _____ Date _____

Mathematics

Ratios

Arithmetic and Number Concepts

DIRECTIONS: Use the table for the example and questions 1–4.

Animal	Number of Students
Sea Lion	6 students
Penguin	14 students
Turtle	11 students
Hammerhead Shark	9 students

1. Which of the following is *not* the ratio of students who saw sea lions to those who saw turtles?
   - (A) $\frac{6}{11}$
   - (B) 6 to 11
   - (C) 6 − 11
   - (D) 6:11

2. What is the ratio of students who saw sea lions to those who saw penguins?
   - (F) 14:6
   - (G) 6 to 20
   - (H) 14:20
   - (J) $\frac{6}{14}$

3. What is the ratio of students who saw turtles to those who saw penguins?
   - (A) 14 to 11
   - (B) $\frac{11}{14}$
   - (C) 11 to 25
   - (D) 14:25

4. What is the ratio of students who saw hammerhead sharks to those who saw penguins?
   - (F) 9:14
   - (G) 9:43
   - (H) 14:9
   - (J) 1:2

DIRECTIONS: For questions 5–7, suppose you had 5 apples, 8 oranges, and 2 bananas.

5. What fraction of the fruit would the apples be?
   - (A) $\frac{5}{10}$
   - (B) $\frac{1}{5}$
   - (C) $\frac{1}{15}$
   - (D) $\frac{1}{3}$

6. What fraction of the fruit would the oranges be?
   - (F) $\frac{8}{7}$
   - (G) $\frac{8}{15}$
   - (H) $\frac{1}{2}$
   - (J) $\frac{8}{5}$

7. What is the ratio of apples to bananas?
   - (A) 5:2
   - (B) $\frac{5}{7}$
   - (C) 5 to 8
   - (D) $\frac{1}{3}$

STOP

Name _____ Date _____

Mathematics
1.T

Proportions

Arithmetic and Number Concepts

DIRECTIONS: Choose the best answer.

1. $\dfrac{3}{\square} = \dfrac{18}{36}$

   - (A) 5
   - (B) 6
   - (C) 8
   - (D) 4

2. $\dfrac{5}{n} = \dfrac{20}{36}$

   - (F) $n = 36$
   - (G) $n = 7$
   - (H) $n = 9$
   - (J) $n = 4$

3. $\dfrac{4}{\square} = \dfrac{24}{42}$

   - (A) 7
   - (B) 20
   - (C) 14
   - (D) 6

4. Which of these numbers can go in the square to make this number sentence true?

   $$\dfrac{1}{\square} > \dfrac{1}{3}$$

   - (F) 2
   - (G) 3
   - (H) 6
   - (J) 5

5. Two triangles are similar. On one triangle, the sides are 4, 5, and 6 units long. The second triangle has sides 8, 10, and x. Use proportions to find x.

   - (A) 14
   - (B) 6
   - (C) 12
   - (D) 10

6. Find n. $\dfrac{1}{8} = \dfrac{n}{16}$

   - (F) 4
   - (G) 8
   - (H) 2
   - (J) 6

7. Find n. $\dfrac{3}{5} = \dfrac{6}{n}$

   - (A) 10
   - (B) 6
   - (C) 3
   - (D) 30

8. Find n. $\dfrac{12}{n} = \dfrac{1}{3}$

   - (F) 6
   - (G) 4
   - (H) 13
   - (J) 36

9. Find n. $\dfrac{n}{27} = \dfrac{6}{18}$

   - (A) 15
   - (B) 3
   - (C) 9
   - (D) 12

10. Find n. $\dfrac{10}{n} = \dfrac{2}{5}$

    - (F) 15
    - (G) 30
    - (H) 25
    - (J) 20

Mathematics 1.U — Using Ratios and Proportions

Arithmetic and Number Concepts

DIRECTIONS: Choose the best answer.

1. "Now batting for Toledo, Mickey Calavito," the game announcer yells into his microphone. In the last game, Mickey got 1 hit in 4 tries. If he continues to hit at this rate, determine how many hits Mickey can expect to get if he bats 600 times during the season.

   - (A) 60 hits
   - (B) 150 hits
   - (C) 160 hits
   - (D) 400 hits

2. The blistering sun shines on a large tree and a small tree that are standing side by side. The large tree casts a shadow of 30 feet, and the small tree casts a 15-foot shadow. If the small tree is 12 feet tall, what is the height of the large tree?

   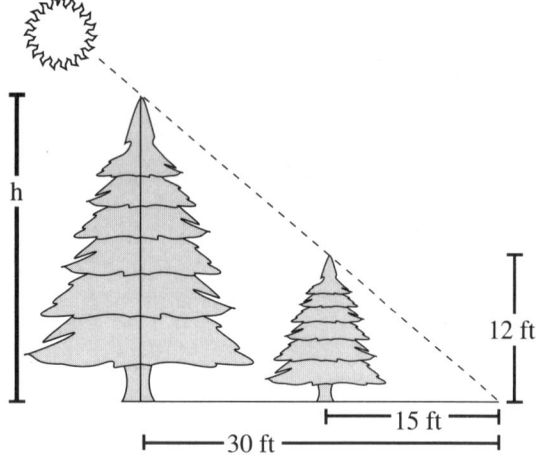

   - (F) 6 feet
   - (G) 15 feet
   - (H) 24 feet
   - (J) 37.5 feet

3. Matilda created this chart when her class had a birthday party for her. Kids brought popsicles, snow cones, ice-cream cones, and quite a few chocolate-covered bananas. The chart shows how many of each type of dessert was eaten at the party. Matilda used her findings to help her mother decide how much of each dessert to make for her brother's birthday party. His party included all 96 people in the sixth grade. Based on the information in the chart, how many ice-cream cones did Matilda's mother make for Matilda's brother's birthday party?

Desserts Kids Like	
Number of Kids	Dessert
7	Ice-cream cones
5	Snow cones
8	Popsicles
1	Chocolate-covered bananas

   - (A) 12 ice-cream cones
   - (B) 14 ice-cream cones
   - (C) 23 ice-cream cones
   - (D) 32 ice-cream cones

4. 12 people are headed down the Colorado River on a rafting trip. In the boat, there are 4 women, 2 men, 2 boys, and 4 girls. If the person who steers the raft is selected at random (these tours are not insured), what is the probability of selecting a boy?

   - (F) $\frac{1}{2}$
   - (G) $\frac{1}{3}$
   - (H) $\frac{1}{4}$
   - (J) $\frac{1}{6}$

STOP

Name _____ Date _____

Mathematics

1.0

For pages 66–90

Mini-Test 1

Arithmetic and Number Concepts

DIRECTIONS: Choose the best answer.

1. Which digit means ten thousands in the numeral 5,873,096?
   - (A) 8
   - (B) 3
   - (C) 7
   - (D) 0

2. Which of these is a composite number?
   - (F) 13
   - (G) 31
   - (H) 59
   - (J) 15

3. Which of these is another way to write 606,344?
   - (A) 60 + 63 + 44
   - (B) 60,000 + 6,000 + 300 + 40 + 4
   - (C) 600,000 + 6,000 + 300 + 40 + 4
   - (D) 600,000 + 60,000 + 300 + 40 + 4

4. What is 0.465 rounded to the nearest tenth?
   - (F) 0.5
   - (G) 0.7
   - (H) 0.6
   - (J) 0.05

5. $\sqrt{36}$
   - (A) 12
   - (B) 3
   - (C) 6
   - (D) 360

6. What number completes this number sentence?

   4 × 35 = 4 × (□ + 5)
   - (F) 35
   - (G) 30
   - (H) 3
   - (J) 38

7. 98,788
   − 23,865
   - (A) 67,765
   - (B) 74,923
   - (C) 77,675
   - (D) None of the above

8. $540.56 + $467.48 =
   - (F) $1,008.04
   - (G) $987.65
   - (H) $1,109.08
   - (J) None of the above

9. $35\overline{)4565}$
   - (A) 160R5
   - (B) 130R15
   - (C) 171
   - (D) None of the above

10. $\frac{4}{9} + \frac{5}{6} =$
    - (F) $1\frac{1}{3}$
    - (G) $1\frac{5}{18}$
    - (H) $1\frac{4}{9}$
    - (J) None of the above

GO

11. $1\frac{5}{8}$
    $\times\ 2\frac{3}{4}$

   A) $4\frac{15}{32}$
   B) $4\frac{3}{8}$
   C) $5\frac{1}{4}$
   D) None of the above

12. 567 × 492 =
   F) 378,964
   G) 216,877
   H) 458,443
   J) None of the above

13. 6.54 ÷ 3 =
   A) 1.9
   B) 2.18
   C) 2.9
   D) None of the above

DIRECTIONS: Choose the best answer. Use the number line for questions 14 and 15.

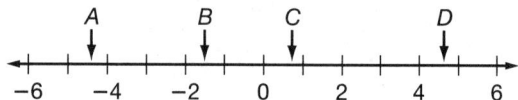

14. Which letter marks $4\frac{6}{10}$ on this number line?
   F) A
   G) B
   H) C
   J) D

15. Which letter marks 0.8 on this number line?
   A) A
   B) B
   C) C
   D) D

DIRECTIONS: Choose the best answer.

16. During the sale, ladies' coats are selling for 75% of the original price. The original price is $98. What is the sale price of the coats?
   F) $24.50
   G) $73.50
   H) $98.00
   J) $75.00

17. Find *n*.
    $$\frac{48}{n} = \frac{2}{4}$$
   A) 24
   B) 96
   C) 12
   D) 36

18. Fred is drawing a scale model of a room that is 12 feet by 14 feet. If he makes one side of the room 3 inches, how long should the other side be?
   F) 4 inches
   G) 14 inches
   H) 3.5 inches
   J) 7 inches

DIRECTIONS: Use this information for questions 19 and 20: There are 4 apples, 2 bananas, 5 oranges, and 3 pears in a fruit bowl.

19. What is the ratio of apples to oranges?
   A) 5:4
   B) $\frac{4}{5}$
   C) 4 to 14
   D) $\frac{9}{5}$

20. What is *not* the ratio of bananas to fruit?
   F) 2 to 14
   G) 2:12
   H) $\frac{1}{7}$
   J) 1:7

92

Mathematics Standards

2.0 Geometry and Measurement Concepts

By the end of the school year, students should:

2.A Measure a given line segment with a standard ruler to the nearest 1 in., $\frac{1}{2}$ in., $\frac{1}{4}$ in., $\frac{1}{8}$ in. *(See page 94.)*

2.B Be familiar with prefixes milli, centi, kilo, and symbols g, mg, kg, mL, L, mm, km, and cm. *(See pages 95–96.)*

2.C Relate metric units to customary units via approximations. *(See page 97.)*

2.D Convert hours and minutes to minutes and perform operations with measures. *(See page 98.)*

2.E Measure the area and perimeter of triangles, squares, rectangles, parallelograms, and irregular polygons. *(See pages 99–100.)*

2.F Understand and use formulas for the circumference and the area of a circle. *(See page 101.)*

2.G Understand the difference between line and point graphs. *(See page 102.)*

2.H Measure angles by using a protractor.

2.I Identify acute, right, obtuse, and straight angles. *(See page 103.)*

2.J Classify triangles according to their sides and according to their angles. *(See page 104.)*

2.K Construct angles given specific angular size in degrees using a protractor.

2.L Construct plane figures using rulers, protractors, and compasses.

2.M Compare plane figures with solid figures. *(See page 105.)*

2.N Recognize differences among solid figures. *(See pages 105–106.)*

2.O Classify two- and three-dimensional shapes according to their properties. *(See pages 106–109.)*

2.P Investigate similar and congruent polygons. *(See page 110.)*

2.Q Understand the concept of parallel and perpendicular lines. *(See page 111.)*

2.R Find the volume of rectangular prisms using cubic units. *(See page 112.)*

2.S Recognize illustrations drawn to scale.

2.T Interpret scale drawings. *(See page 113.)*

Name _____ Date _____

Mathematics

Measuring With a Ruler

Geometry and Measurement Concepts

DIRECTIONS: Follow the instructions with each question for measuring the line segments.

1. What is the length of the line below to the nearest inch? _____

   ————————————————————————

2. What is the length of the line below to the nearest 1/2 inch? _____

   ————————————————

3. What is the length of the line below to the nearest 1/4 inch? _____

   ——————————————————————

4. What is the length of the line below to the nearest 1/8 inch? _____

   ————————————

5. What is the length of the line below to the nearest inch? _____

   ——————————————————

6. What is the length of the line below to the nearest 1/2 inch? _____

   —————————

7. What is the length of the line above to the nearest 1/4 inch? _____

   ———————————— .

8. What is the length of the line below to the nearest 1/8 inch? _____

   ————————————————————

Name _____ Date _____

Mathematics
2.B

Capacity Measurements–Metric

Geometry and Measurement Concepts

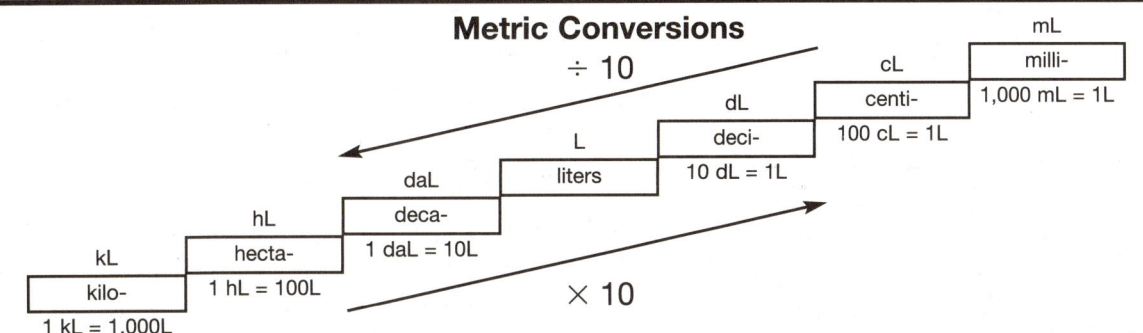

Metric Conversions

÷ 10

kL kilo- 1 kL = 1,000L
hL hecta- 1 hL = 100L
daL deca- 1 daL = 10L
L liters
dL deci- 10 dL = 1L
cL centi- 100 cL = 1L
mL milli- 1,000 mL = 1L

× 10

Multiply when moving up on the chart—from kiloliters to liters or from liters to centiliters. Divide when moving down on the chart—from milliliters to deciliters or from meters to hectaliters.

Smaller Units to Larger Units	Larger Units to Smaller Units
5,700 mL = _____ L	_____ cL = 7.38 hL
To get from milliliters to liters you must move down three stairs. So, divide by 10^3 (or 1,000).	To get from hectaliters to centiliters you must move up 4 stairs. So, multiply by 10^4 (or 10,000).
5,700 mL ÷ 1,000 = 5.7 L	7.38 hL × 10,000 = 73,800 cL

DIRECTIONS: Use the chart to help you convert the metric units.

1. 16 dL = _____ mL
2. 162,100 mL = _____ hL
3. 8.9 daL = _____ dL
4. 16 kL = _____ mL
5. 9 L = _____ hL
6. 16.8 hL = _____ cL
7. 0.06 hL = _____ mL
8. 0.08 L = _____ cL
9. 0.06 daL = _____ cL

DIRECTIONS: Compare the following measurements using <, >, or =.

10. 296 mL _____ 3 L
11. 11.61 hL _____ 11,000 dL
12. 5 kL _____ 5,000 L

95

Mass Measurements–Metric

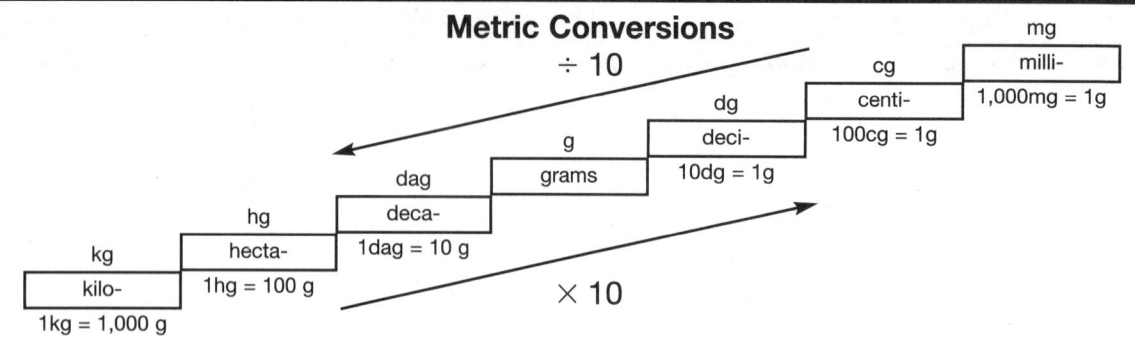

Multiply when moving up on the chart—from kiloliters to liters or from liters to centiliters. Divide when moving down on the chart—from milliliters to deciliters or from meters to hectoliters.

Smaller Units to Larger Units
6,095 mg = _____ g
To get from milligrams to grams you must move down three stairs. So, divide by 10^3 (or 1,000).
6,095 mg ÷ 1,000 = 6.095 g

Larger Units to Smaller Units
_____ cg = 7.52 hg
To get from hectagrams to centigrams you must move up 4 stairs. So, multiply by 10^4 (or 10,000).
7.52 hg × 10,000 = 75,200 cg

DIRECTIONS: Use the chart to help you convert the metric units.

1. 7.2 kg = _____ dg
2. 11.01 g = _____ mg
3. 16.013 kg = _____ dag
4. 0.062 g = _____ cg
5. 310 hg = _____ g
6. 0.013 cg = _____ hg
7. 21.9 dag = _____ kg
8. 0.121 cg = _____ dg
9. 11.61 hg = _____ dg

DIRECTIONS: Compare the following measurements using <, >, or =.

10. 6.2 kg _____ 5,000 g
11. 12,437 mg _____ 1.2437 dag
12. 79 dg _____ 9 g

Mathematics 2.C

Relating Metric Units to Customary Units

Geometry and Measurement Concepts

---

1 mile = 1.6 kilometer
1 kilogram = 2.2 pounds

Smaller Units to Larger Units	**Larger Units to Smaller Units**
74.8 lb. = _____ kg	14 mi. = _____ km
1 kg = 2.2 lb.	1 mi. = 1.6 km
74.8 ÷ 2.2 = 34	x 14 x 14
74.8 lb. = 34 kg	14 mi. = 22.4 km

DIRECTIONS: Convert the following measurements.

1. 3 mi. = _____ km

2. 12 lb. = _____ kg

3. 8 km = _____ mi.

4. 6.6 lb. = _____ kg

5. 210 lb. = _____ kg

6. 10 mi. = _____ km

7. 3.2 km = _____ mi.

8. 9.6 km = _____ mi.

9. 79.2 lb. = _____ kg

DIRECTIONS: Compare the following measurements using <, >, or =.

10. 50 lb. _____ 23 kg

11. 9 mi. _____ 13 km

12. 7 mi. _____ 11.2 km

Name _____ Date _____

Mathematics
2.D

Time Measurement

Geometry and Measurement Concepts

DIRECTIONS: Choose the answer that shows the elapsed time for each problem.

1. 9:59 in the morning to 2:59 in the afternoon
   - (A) 7 hours
   - (B) 5 hours
   - (C) 3 hours
   - (D) 1 hour

2. five in the afternoon to 1 minute after midnight
   - (F) 5 hours 1 minute
   - (G) 6 hours
   - (H) 7 hours 1 minute
   - (J) 7 hours

3. 1:57 A.M. to 10:43 A.M.
   - (A) 3 hours 14 minutes
   - (B) 4 hours 5 minutes
   - (C) 10 hours 40 minutes
   - (D) 8 hours 46 minutes

4. 1:01 A.M. to 4:29 P.M.
   - (F) 13 hours 28 minutes
   - (G) 15 hours 28 minutes
   - (H) 16 hours 8 minutes
   - (J) 18 hours 32 minutes

5. fifty-three minutes after seven in the morning to 11:38 A.M.
   - (A) 3 hours 45 minutes
   - (B) 4 hours 45 minutes
   - (C) 12 hours 45 minutes
   - (D) 15 hours 45 minutes

DIRECTIONS: Choose the best answer.

6. How many minutes are in $3\frac{1}{4}$ hours?
   - (F) 300 minutes
   - (G) 195 minutes
   - (H) 180 minutes
   - (J) 225 minutes

7. How many minutes are in $2\frac{1}{3}$ hours?
   - (A) 120 minutes
   - (B) 130 minutes
   - (C) 140 minutes
   - (D) 133 minutes

8. How many minutes are in $4\frac{1}{4}$ hours?
   - (F) 240 minutes
   - (G) 245 minutes
   - (H) 250 minutes
   - (J) 255 minutes

9. Travis got on the school bus as 8:45 A.M. and returned home at 3:30 P.M. How many minutes was he gone from home?
   - (A) 405 minutes
   - (B) 345 minutes
   - (C) 430 minutes
   - (D) 445 minutes

10. Keisha practices swimming every Thursday from 3:45 P.M. to 5:00 P.M. How many minutes does she practice?
    - (F) 65 minutes
    - (G) 75 minutes
    - (H) 70 minutes
    - (J) 45 minutes

Name _____ Date _____

Mathematics
2.E

Area and Perimeter of Polygons

Geometry and Measurement Concepts

DIRECTIONS: Find the area and perimeter of each polygon below. Include the correct units in your answers.

Examples:

Triangle: Area = $\frac{1}{2}bh$ b = base

Rectangle: Area = bh h = height

Parallelogram: Area = bh

Trapezoid: Area = $\frac{1}{2}h(\text{base 1} + \text{base 2})$

Remember, the base and height must be perpendicular.
To find the perimeter of any shape, add the lengths of all sides.

1.

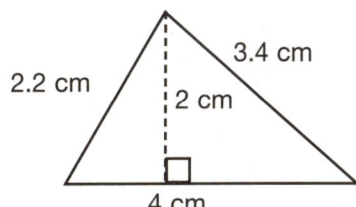

Area: _____

Perimeter: _____

2.

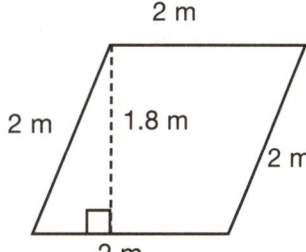

Area: _____

Perimeter: _____

3.

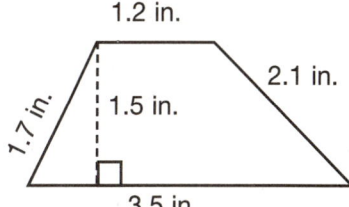

Area: _____

Perimeter: _____

4.

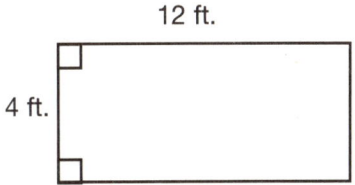

Area: _____

Perimeter: _____

5.

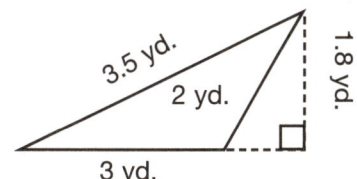

Area: _____

Perimeter: _____

6.

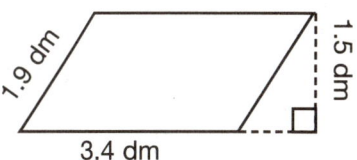

Area: _____

Perimeter: _____

STOP

Name _____ Date _____

Mathematics
2.E

Area of Irregular Shapes

Geometry and Measurement Concepts

DIRECTIONS: Find the area of each shape. Include the correct units in your answer.

Example:

Irregular spaces can be divided into common shapes, such as rectangles and right triangles, as shown in the diagram below. If you find the area of each small shape using rules, you can add their areas together to find the area of the large shape.

Region 1 = $\frac{1}{2}$ bh = $\frac{1}{2}$ × 2 × 2.5 = 2.5 m²

Region 2 = bh = 3 × 2.5 = 7.5 m²

Region 3 = bh = 1.5 × 1.7 = 2.55 m²

+ Region 4 = $\frac{1}{2}$ bh = $\frac{1}{2}$ × 1 × 1.7 = 0.85 m²

Total Area = 13.4 m²

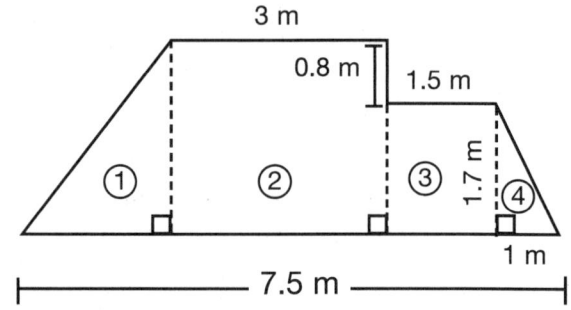

1.
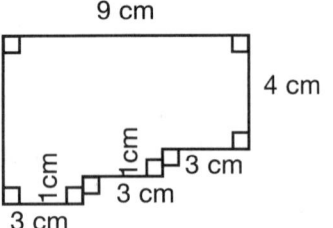

Area: _____

2.
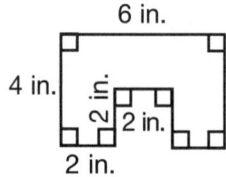

Area: _____

3.
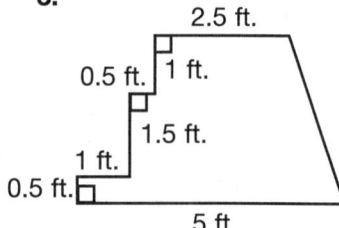

Area: _____

4.
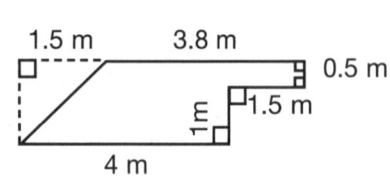

Area: _____

5.
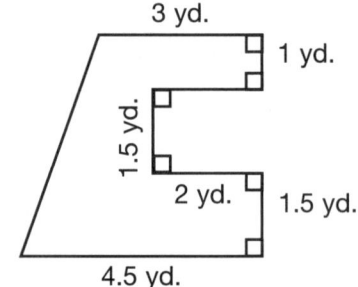

Area: _____

STOP

100

Name _____ Date _____

Mathematics

2.F

Circumference and Area of Circles

Geometry and Measurement Concepts

DIRECTIONS: Find the circumference and area of each circle below. Include the appropriate units in your answer.

Example:

The **circumference** of a circle is the distance around the outside of the circle.
$C = \pi d$, where d = diameter

The **area** of a circle is the space inside the circle.
$A = \pi r^2$, where r = radius

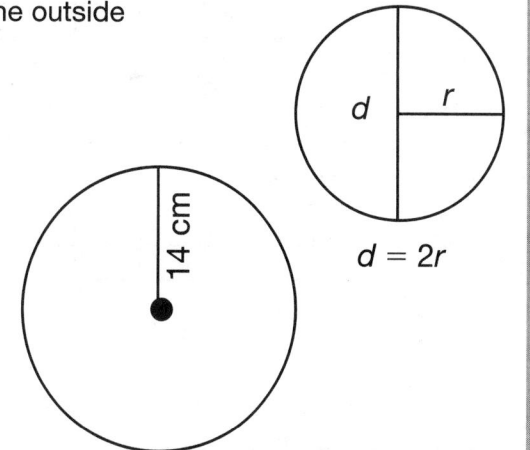

$\pi = 3.14$

$d = 2r = 2 \times 14 = 28$ cm
$C = \pi d = 3.14 \times 28 = 87.92$ cm
$A = \pi r^2 = 3.14 \times 14^2 = 3.14 \times 196 = 615.44$ cm^2

1.
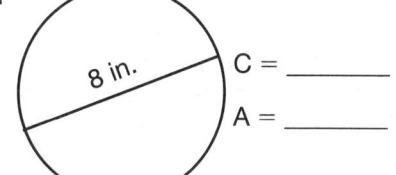
8 in.
C = _____
A = _____

2.
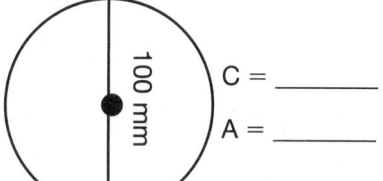
100 mm
C = _____
A = _____

3.
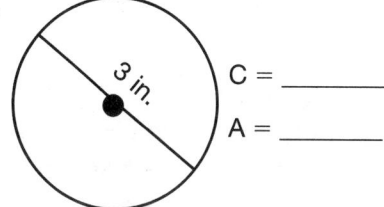
3 in.
C = _____
A = _____

4.
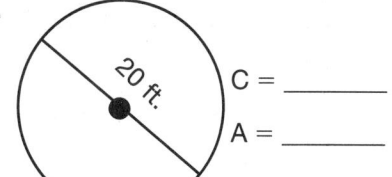
20 ft.
C = _____
A = _____

5.
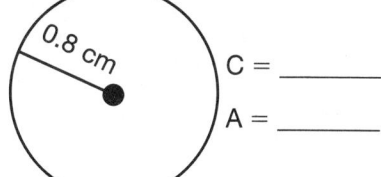
0.8 cm
C = _____
A = _____

6.
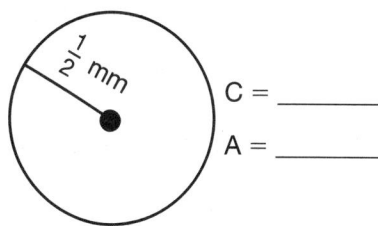
$\frac{1}{2}$ mm
C = _____
A = _____

7.
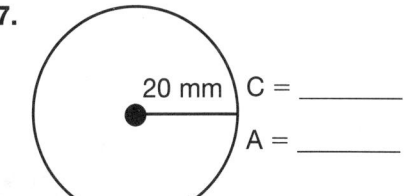
20 mm
C = _____
A = _____

8.
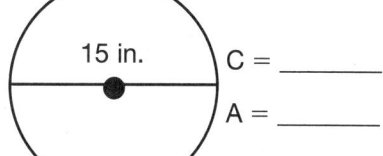
15 in.
C = _____
A = _____

9.
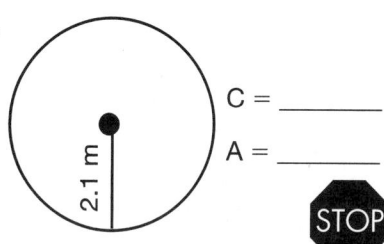
2.1 m
C = _____
A = _____

STOP

101

Name _____ Date _____

Mathematics
2.G

Line and Point Graphs

Geometry and Measurement Concepts

DIRECTIONS: The graph below shows the average basketball attendance for the season. Use the graph to answer questions 1–3.

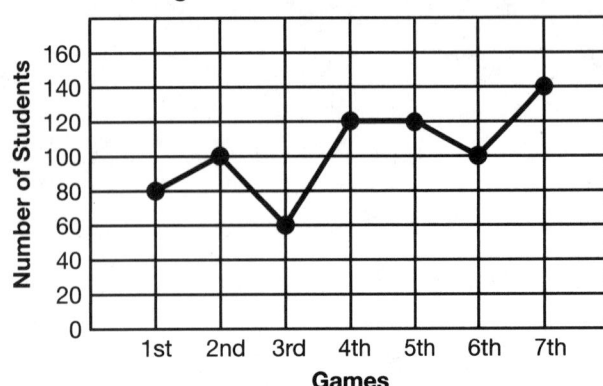

1. What was the increase in attendance from the first to the seventh game?

   - (A) 50 students
   - (B) 60 students
   - (C) 140 students
   - (D) 70 students

2. Between which two games was there the smallest increase in attendance?

   - (F) 1st and 2nd games
   - (G) 6th and 7th games
   - (H) 5th and 6th games
   - (J) 2nd and 3rd games

3. How many students all together attended games?

   - (A) 140 students
   - (B) 160 students
   - (C) 720 students
   - (D) 600 students

DIRECTIONS: Study the graph below, and then answer numbers 4–6.

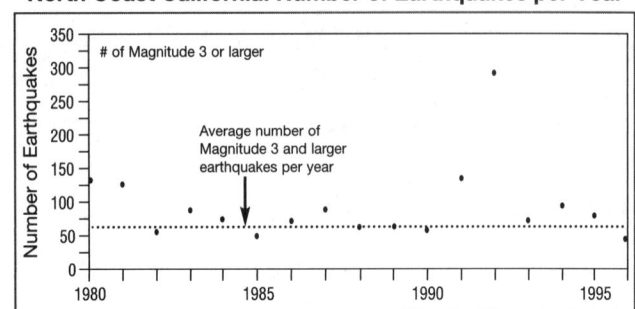

4. In what year did the greatest number of earthquakes occur?

   - (F) 1990
   - (G) 1991
   - (H) 1992
   - (J) 1993

5. In what year did the fewest number of earthquakes occur?

   - (A) 1981
   - (B) 1986
   - (C) 1991
   - (D) 1996

6. Based on the data, what is an average number of earthquakes per year on the North Coast of California?

   - (F) about 250
   - (G) about 150
   - (H) about 100
   - (J) about 50

STOP

Name _____ Date _____

Mathematics
2.1

Identifying Angles

Geometry and
Measurement
Concepts

DIRECTIONS: Find each of the angles on the figure shown below. For each angle, write the letter R, S, O, or A if the angle is right, straight, obtuse, or acute.

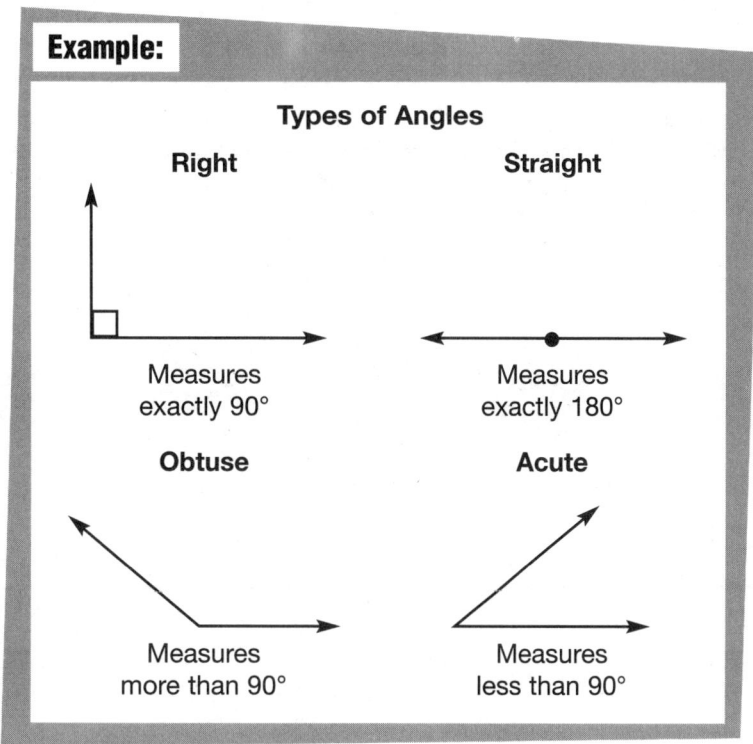

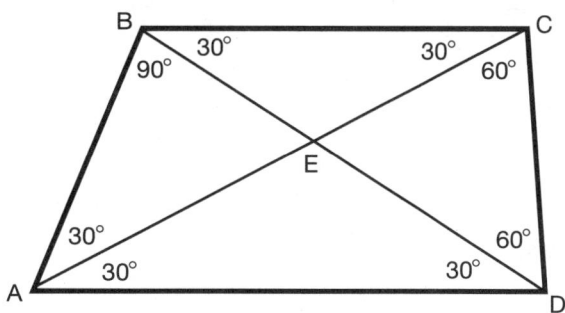

_____ 1. ∠ ECB   _____ 5. ∠ AEC   _____ 9. ∠ DEB

_____ 2. ∠ ABC   _____ 6. ∠ CDE   _____ 10. ∠ CEB

_____ 3. ∠ AED   _____ 7. ∠ ABE

_____ 4. ∠ CDA   _____ 8. ∠ BAE

103

Name _____   Date _____

Mathematics
2.J

Classifying Triangles

Geometry and Measurement Concepts

DIRECTIONS: Look at each triangle. Write the type of triangle (*right, acute,* or *obtuse*) on the line. Then, write the measurement of the missing angle. The first one is done for you.

 The angle measures in a triangle always add up to 180°. A **right** triangle has one 90° angle. An **obtuse** triangle has one angle that is greater than 90°. An **acute** triangle has all three angles less than 90°.

1. 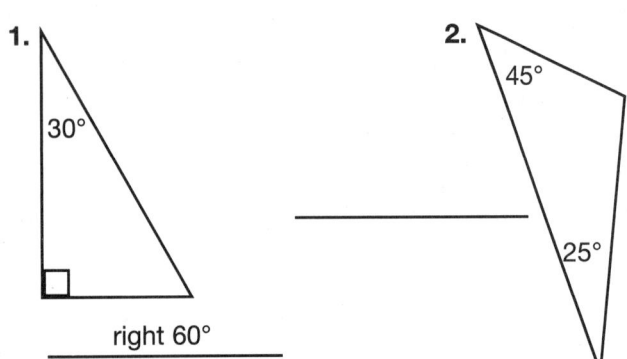 right 60°

2.

3.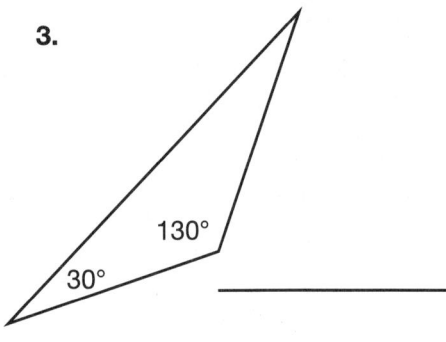

4.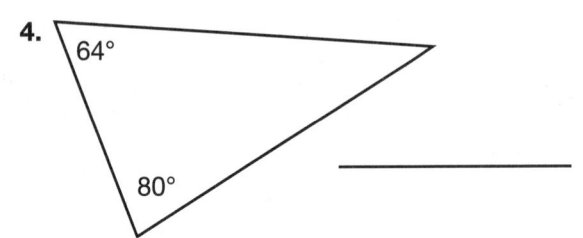

5.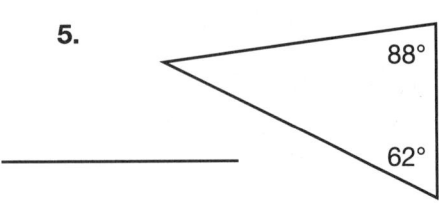

6.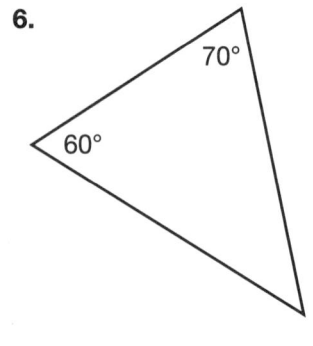

7.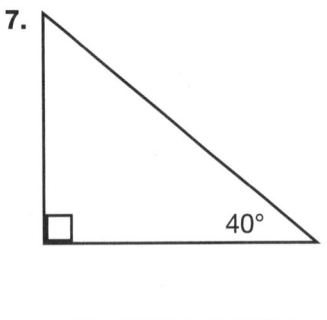

8.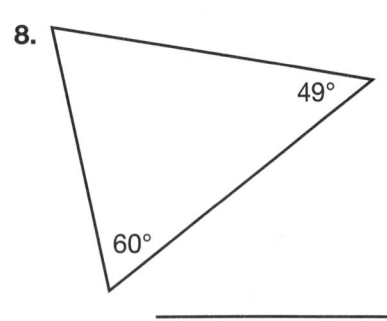

Name _____ Date _____

Mathematics
2.M

Comparing Plane Figures With Solid Figures

Geometry and Measurement Concepts

DIRECTIONS: The figures on the left show representations of solid figures. The figures on the right show the plane representations of the solid figures. Draw a line from each solid figure on the left to its plane figure on the right.

Solid Figures   **Plane Figures**

1.    A.

2. 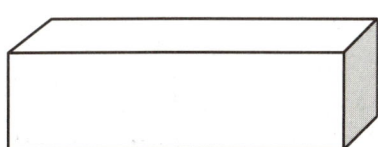   B.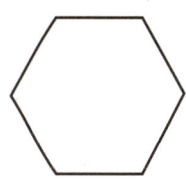

3. 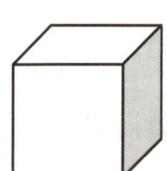   C.

4. 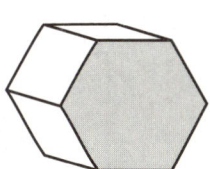   D.

5.    E.

105

Name _____ Date _____

Mathematics
2.0

Classifying Polygons

Geometry and Measurement Concepts

DIRECTIONS: Write the name of each polygon.

1.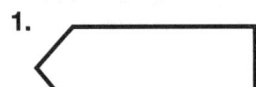
_____

2.
_____

Polygon Name	Number of Sides
Triangle	3
Quadrilateral	4
Pentagon	5
Hexagon	6
Heptagon	7
Octagon	8
Decagon	10
Dodecagon	12
13-gon	13

3.
_____

4.
_____

5.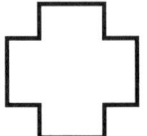
_____

6.
_____

7.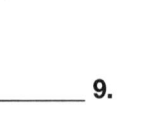
_____

8.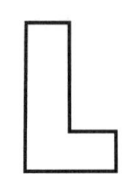
_____

DIRECTIONS: Write the letter of the correct polygon name on the blank next to the matching shape.

Polygon Name

a. triangle

b. quadrilateral

c. pentagon

d. hexagon

e. heptagon

f. octagon

____ 9.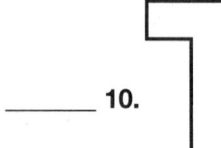

____ 10.

____ 11.

____ 12.

____ 13.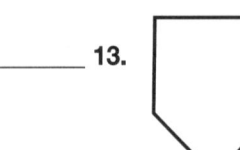

____ 14.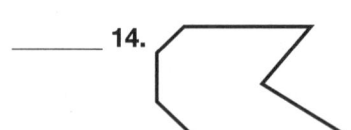

STOP

Name _____ Date _____

Mathematics 2.0

Classifying Quadrilaterals

Geometry and Measurement Concepts

DIRECTIONS: Give the name for each quadrilateral. Then, find each missing angle measurement.

Name	Description	Example
trapezoid	• 1 pair of opposite sides are parallel	
parallelogram	• opposite sides are parallel • opposite sides and opposite angles are congruent	
rhombus	• parallelogram with all sides congruent	
rectangle	• parallelogram with four right angles	
square	• rectangle with four congruent sides	

Clue: The sum of the measures of the angles in any quadrilateral is 360°.

1.

_____

2.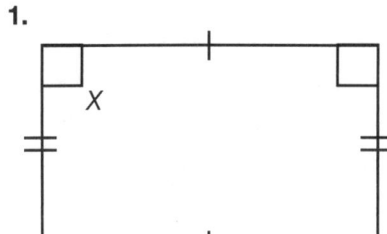

_____

3.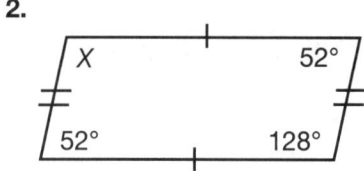

_____

4.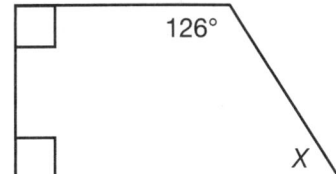

_____

5.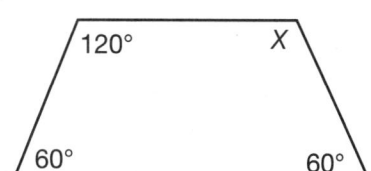

_____

6.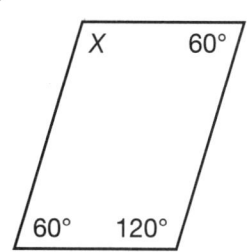

_____

107

Name _____ Date _____

Mathematics
2.0

Classifying Polyhedrons

Geometry and Measurement Concepts

DIRECTIONS: Next to each shape below, write *prism, pyramid,* or *neither* to show what type of 3-dimensional object it is. Be prepared to explain your answers.

Examples:

Prisms are 3-dimensional shapes with the following characteristics:
- two opposite, identical bases shaped like polygons
- rectangular faces

Pyramids are 3-dimensional shapes with the following characteristics:
- one base shaped like a polygon
- triangular faces
- a point on one end

1. 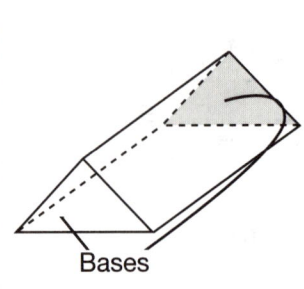 _____

2. 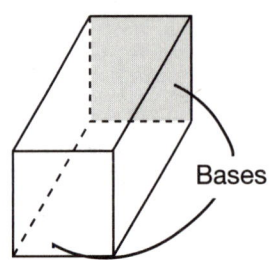 _____

3. 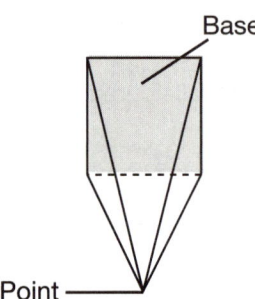 _____

4. 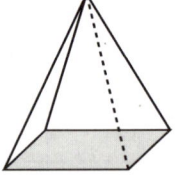 _____

5. 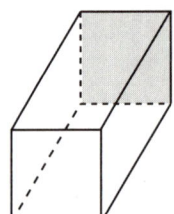 _____

6. 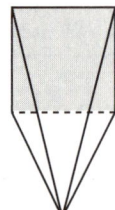 _____

7. 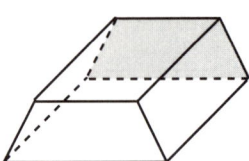 _____

8. 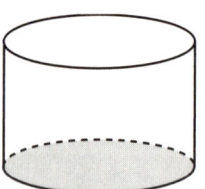 _____

9. 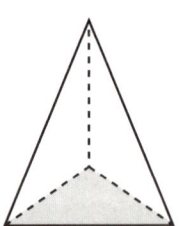 _____

108

Name _____ Date _____

Mathematics
2.0

Cylinders, Cones, and Spheres

Geometry and Measurement Concepts

DIRECTIONS: Many everyday objects contain these shapes. For each object shown below, write *cone, cylinder, sphere,* or *none of these* near the objects that resemble those shapes.

Examples:

A **cone** is a 3-dimensional shape with a circular base, a curved surface, and one point, or vertex.

A **cylinder** is a 3-dimensional shape with two circular bases and a curved surface.

A **sphere** is a completely curved 3-dimensional shape.

1.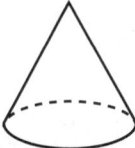
   _____

2.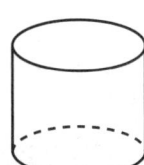
   _____

3.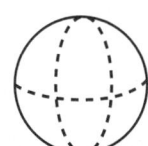
   _____

4.
   _____

5.
   _____

6.
   _____

7.
   _____

8.
   _____

9.
   _____

10.
    _____

11.
    _____

12.
    _____

STOP

109

Name _____ Date _____

Mathematics

Similar and Congruent Figures

Geometry and Measurement Concepts

DIRECTIONS: Write congruent or similar below each set of shapes.

 **Congruent** shapes are the same size and shape.
Similar shapes are the same shape, but not the same size.

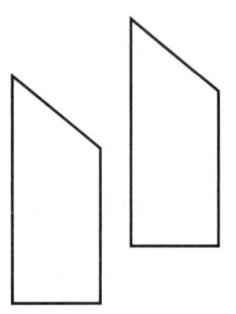　　　　

1. _____　2. _____　3. _____

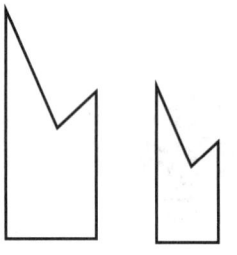　　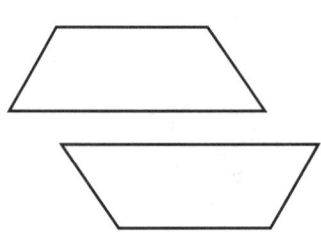　　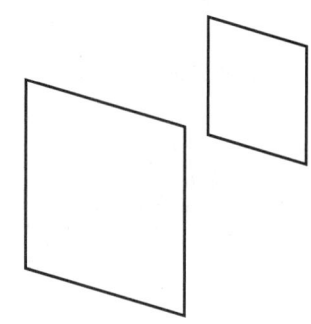

4. _____　5. _____　6. _____

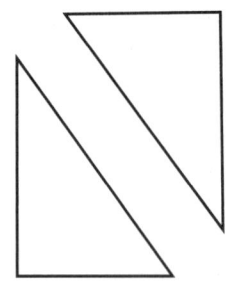　　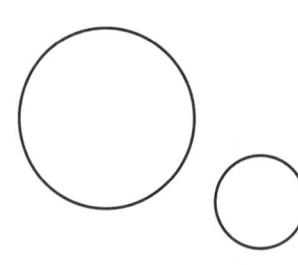　　

7. _____　8. _____　9. _____

Name _____ Date _____

Mathematics
2.Q

Parallel and Perpendicular Lines

Geometry and Measurement Concepts

DIRECTIONS: Tell whether each pair of lines is *parallel, perpendicular,* or *neither*.

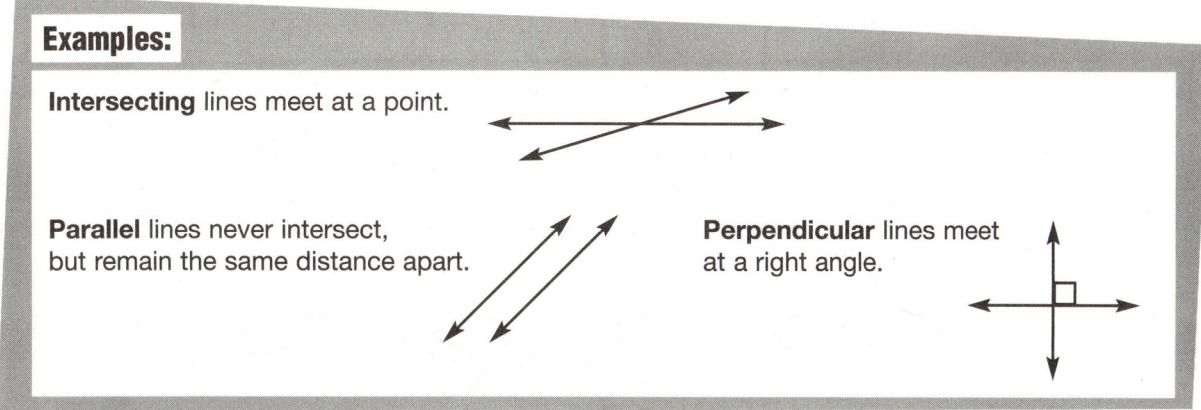

Examples:

Intersecting lines meet at a point.

Parallel lines never intersect, but remain the same distance apart.

Perpendicular lines meet at a right angle.

1. $\overleftrightarrow{QR}$ and $\overleftrightarrow{RT}$ _____
2. $\overleftrightarrow{RT}$ and $\overleftrightarrow{SU}$ _____
3. $\overleftrightarrow{SU}$ and $\overleftrightarrow{PQ}$ _____
4. $\overleftrightarrow{PQ}$ and $\overleftrightarrow{RT}$ _____
5. $\overleftrightarrow{PQ}$ and $\overleftrightarrow{QR}$ _____

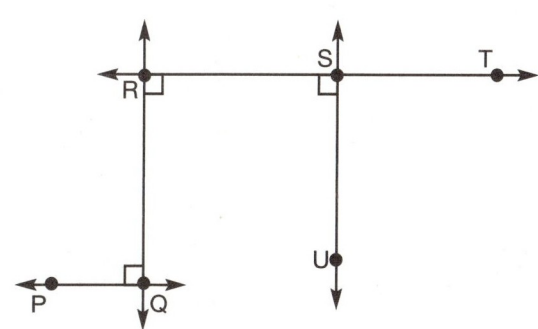

DIRECTIONS: Tell whether each pair of lines is *parallel, perpendicular,* or *neither*.

6. $\overleftrightarrow{AC}$ and $\overleftrightarrow{DE}$ _____
7. $\overleftrightarrow{CE}$ and $\overleftrightarrow{CF}$ _____
8. $\overleftrightarrow{CF}$ and $\overleftrightarrow{AC}$ _____
9. $\overleftrightarrow{CF}$ and $\overleftrightarrow{AD}$ _____
10. $\overleftrightarrow{DF}$ and $\overleftrightarrow{AD}$ _____
11. $\overleftrightarrow{BD}$ and $\overleftrightarrow{BC}$ _____
12. $\overleftrightarrow{DF}$ and $\overleftrightarrow{EC}$ _____
13. $\overleftrightarrow{BC}$ and $\overleftrightarrow{AD}$ _____

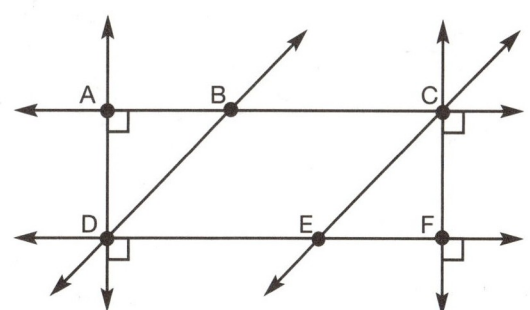

STOP

Name _____ Date _____

Mathematics 2.R

Volume of Rectangular Prisms

Geometry and Measurement Concepts

DIRECTIONS: Find the volume of the following rectangular prisms. Include the appropriate units in your answer.

Example:

Volume of a prism = area of base × height

The base of a rectangular prism is a rectangle.

 Area of a rectangle = length × width

Volume of a rectangular prism
 = length × width × height

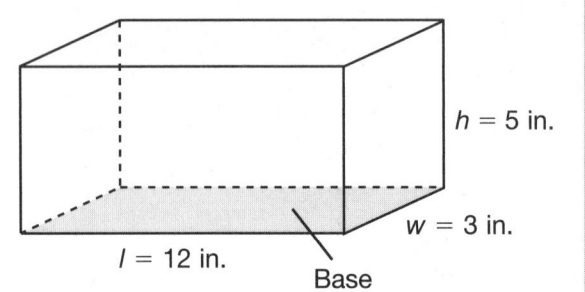

$V = lwh$
$V = 12 \text{ in.} \times 3 \text{ in.} \times 5 \text{ in.} = 36 \times 5 = 180 \text{ in.}^3$

1.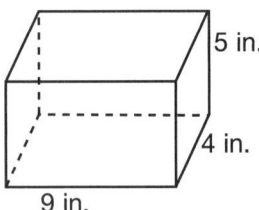

Volume _____

2.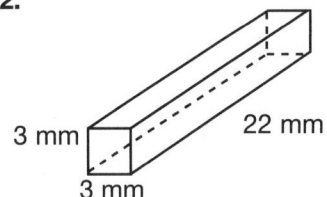

Volume _____

3.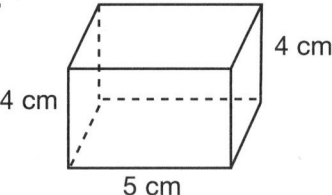

Volume _____

4.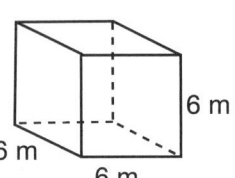

Volume _____

5.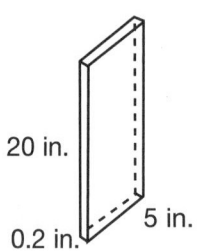

Volume _____

6.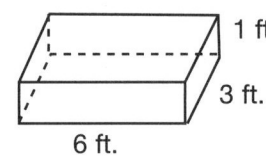

Volume _____

7.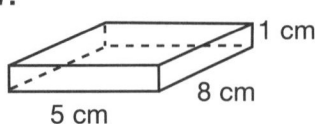

Volume _____

8.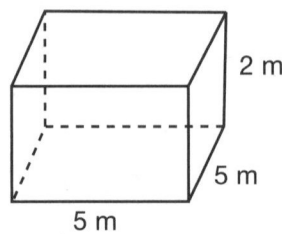

Volume _____

9.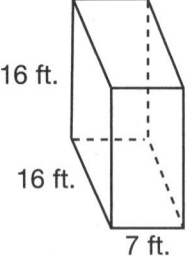

Volume _____

Name _____ Date _____

Mathematics
2.T

Scale Drawings

Geometry and Measurement Concepts

 **Clue** — A scale drawing is a drawing that represents a real object. For example, a map of the United States is a scale drawing that represents the actual United States. The scale of the drawing is the ratio of the size of the drawing to the actual size of the object.

1. Let's imagine that an architect wants to show a scale drawing of a stadium that she is designing. The actual stadium is 100 yards long and 75 yards wide. The architect might make 3 inches represent 25 yards. If she did this, what would be the length and width of the stadium drawn on a sheet of paper?

   _____

2. Make a scale drawing of your classroom or one of the rooms in your house. Use the grid below to make your drawing. Be sure to include what scale you will use to represent the actual room.

STOP

113

Name _____ Date _____

Mathematics

2.0

For pages 94–113

Mini-Test 2

Geometry and Measurement Concepts

DIRECTIONS: Choose the best answer.

1. Lucinda wants to run in the newly created Tampa Bay 10,000. It is a 10,000 meter race. The farthest Lucinda has ever run before is $\frac{1}{2}$ that distance. In kilometers, what is the greatest distance Lucinda has ever run before?

   (A) 5 km
   (B) 10 km
   (C) 50 km
   (D) 1,000 km

2. This fingernail is about 1 centimeter wide. About how many centimeters long is this paper clip?

   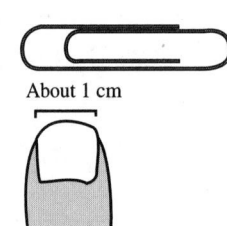

   (F) 1 cm
   (G) 2 cm
   (H) 3 cm
   (J) 4 cm

3. A soccer game started at 11:10 A.M. and lasted $1\frac{1}{2}$ hours. About what time did the game end?

   (A) 12:30 P.M.
   (B) 1:30 P.M.
   (C) 12:00 A.M.
   (D) 1:00 A.M.

4. A triangle with one 90° angle is called _____ .

   (F) isosceles
   (G) scalene
   (H) equilateral
   (J) right

5. Which of the figures below are congruent?

   A   B   C   D

   (A) B and C
   (B) A and C
   (C) B and D
   (D) A and D

6. Which of the angles below is acute?

   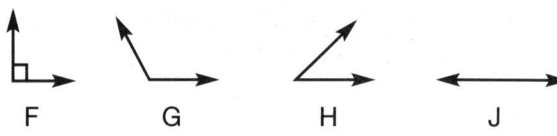
   F   G   H   J

   (F)
   (G)
   (H)
   (J)

7. Which of these is not a cone?

    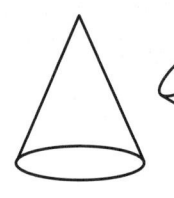 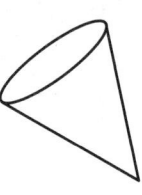 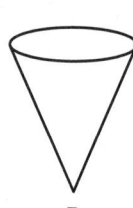
   A   B   C   D

   (A)
   (B)
   (C)
   (D)

GO

114

Name _____ Date _____

DIRECTIONS: Write the letter of the correct polygon name on the blank next to the matching shape.

_____ 8.

_____ 9.

_____ 10.

_____ 11.

_____ 12.

_____ 13.

a. triangle

b. quadrilateral

c. pentagon

d. hexagon

e. heptagon

f. octagon

DIRECTIONS: Choose the best answer.

14. Which of the following lines are parallel?

   (F)

   (G)

   (H)

   (J)

15. What is the area of a classroom that is 17 meters long and 8 meters wide?
    - (A) 50 square meters
    - (B) 136 square meters
    - (C) 25 square meters
    - (D) 9 square meters

16. Bernice measured three circles and came up with the following table. Which of the following statements is true?

Diameter	Circumference
$\frac{1}{3}$ unit	1 unit
1 unit	3 units
2 units	$6\frac{1}{3}$ units

- (F) Diameter times three equals circumference.
- (G) Diameter times a number slightly larger than three equals circumference.
- (H) Diameter times four equals circumference.
- (J) There is no relationship.

17. The scale on a map shows that 1 inch equals 8 miles. About how long would a section of road be that is 2.4 inches on the map?
    - (A) 25 miles
    - (B) 10.5 miles
    - (C) 19 miles
    - (D) 29 miles

STOP

115

Mathematics Standards

3.0 Function and Algebra Concepts
By the end of the school year, students should:

- **3.A** Find succeeding terms in a sequence of numbers (e.g., 1, 3, 6, 10, 15, . . .). *(See page 117.)*
- **3.B** Use fractional notation to show ratios. *(See page 118.)*
- **3.C** Understand ratio and proportion. *(See page 119.)*
- **3.D** Read ordered number pairs on a grid. *(See page 120.)*
- **3.E** Graph ordered number pairs on a grid. *(See page 121.)*
- **3.F** Use ordered pairs to construct figures on a grid. *(See page 122.)*
- **3.G** Develop an understanding of functions and functional relationships that a change in one quantity (variable) results in a change in another. *(See page 123.)*
- **3.H** Apply and explain the order of operations. *(See page 124.)*
- **3.I** Define equivalent open sentences as equations having the same solution set. *(See page 125.)*
- **3.J** Define and recognize open sentences using variable and equal symbols. *(See page 126.)*
- **3.K** Decide whether a number sentence is true or false. *(See page 127.)*
- **3.L** Use the symbols =, <, and > to write true number sentences. *(See page 128.)*
- **3.M** Use letters for variables to write rules for real-life situations. *(See page 129.)*
- **3.N** Develop methods to solve basic linear equations. *(See page 130.)*

Number Sequence

Mathematics 3.A

Function and Algebra Concepts

DIRECTIONS: Fill in the blanks to complete the numerical sequence.

Example:

2, 4, _____, 8, _____, 12

Answer: 6, 10

1. _____, 729, _____, 81, 27, 9

2. 4, 8, 12, 16, _____, _____

3. 21, 42, _____, 84, 105, 126, _____

4. 55, 52, 49, _____, 43, _____

5. 272,820,394; _____; 2,254,714; _____; 18,634; 1,694; 154

6. 23, 46, _____, 92, 115, 138, _____

7. 41,803,776; _____; 290,304; _____; 2,016; 168

8. 25, 50, 75, 100, 125, _____, _____

9. 30, 37, 44, 51, _____, 65, _____

10. 107, 92, _____, 62, 47, _____

11. 2, 4, 8, 16, _____, 64, _____

12. 1, 2, 3, 5, 7, _____, 13, 17, _____

13. 5, 25, _____, 625, _____

14. 2,592, 864, _____, _____, 32

15. 108, 120, 132, _____, _____, 168, 180

117

Name _____ Date _____

Mathematics

3.B **Using Fractions to Show Ratios**

Function and Algebra Concepts

DIRECTIONS: Choose the best answer.

1. Captain Agin wants to paint the deck of his boat. He has a budget for 18 cans of paint—6 red cans, 8 white, and 4 blue. What fraction of the cans of paint will be blue?

   (A) $\frac{4}{18}$ or $\frac{2}{9}$

   (B) $\frac{6}{18}$ or $\frac{2}{6}$

   (C) $\frac{8}{18}$ or $\frac{4}{9}$

   (D) $\frac{18}{36}$ or $\frac{1}{2}$

2. When it rains 3 inches in an hour at Calistoga Creek, the creek rises $\frac{1}{2}$ inch. If the rise of the water in Calistoga Creek is proportional to the amount of rain the creek receives, how much will the creek rise if it rains 8 inches in an hour?

   (F) 24 inches

   (G) $1\frac{1}{2}$ inches

   (H) $1\frac{1}{3}$ inches

   (J) $\frac{3}{16}$ inches

3. The ratio of boys who play kickball at recess to girls who play kickball at recess is 5 to 8. If there are 20 boys playing kickball, how many girls are playing?

   (A) 32 girls

   (B) 40 girls

   (C) 100 girls

   (D) 160 girls

DIRECTIONS: For questions 4–6, suppose you had a glass jar with 6 red, 5 green, 8 blue, and 3 yellow marbles.

4. What fraction of the marbles are red?

   (F) $\frac{2}{11}$

   (G) $\frac{1}{4}$

   (H) $\frac{3}{22}$

   (J) $\frac{3}{11}$

5. What fraction of the marbles are blue?

   (A) $\frac{8}{7}$

   (B) $\frac{4}{11}$

   (C) $\frac{1}{3}$

   (D) $\frac{8}{5}$

6. What is the ratio of yellow marbles to blue marbles?

   (F) $\frac{3}{8}$

   (G) 8:3

   (H) 5 to 8

   (J) $\frac{1}{2}$

STOP

Name _____ Date _____

Mathematics
3.C

Understanding Ratio and Proportion

Function and Algebra Concepts

DIRECTIONS: Choose the best answer.

Example:

What is the ratio of four days to four weeks?

Ⓐ $\frac{1}{14}$

Ⓑ $\frac{1}{7}$

Ⓒ $\frac{1}{2}$

Ⓓ $\frac{1}{15}$

Answer: Ⓑ

Before you choose an answer, ask yourself if the answer makes sense. If you are confused by a problem, read it again. If you are still confused, skip the problem and come back to it later.

1. It takes 5 workers about 50 hours to build a house. How long would it take if there were 10 workers?

   Ⓐ 25 hours
   Ⓑ 12 1/2 hours
   Ⓒ 100 hours
   Ⓓ None of the above

2. The scale on a map shows that 1 inch equals 800 miles. About how long would a section of road be that is 3 inches on the map?

   Ⓕ 2,400 miles
   Ⓖ 240 miles
   Ⓗ 24 miles
   Ⓙ 24,000 miles

3. Suppose you had 6 apples, 6 oranges, and 4 bananas. What fraction of the fruit would the apples be?

   Ⓐ $\frac{6}{15}$ Ⓒ $\frac{3}{4}$

   Ⓑ $\frac{1}{2}$ Ⓓ $\frac{3}{8}$

4. If you added 2 apples and removed 2 bananas, what fraction of the fruit would the bananas be?

   Ⓕ $\frac{1}{3}$ Ⓗ $\frac{2}{5}$

   Ⓖ $\frac{1}{8}$ Ⓙ $\frac{1}{4}$

STOP

Name _____ Date _____

Mathematics
3.D **Reading Ordered Number Pairs**

Function and Algebra Concepts

DIRECTIONS: Use the following grid for questions 1–5.

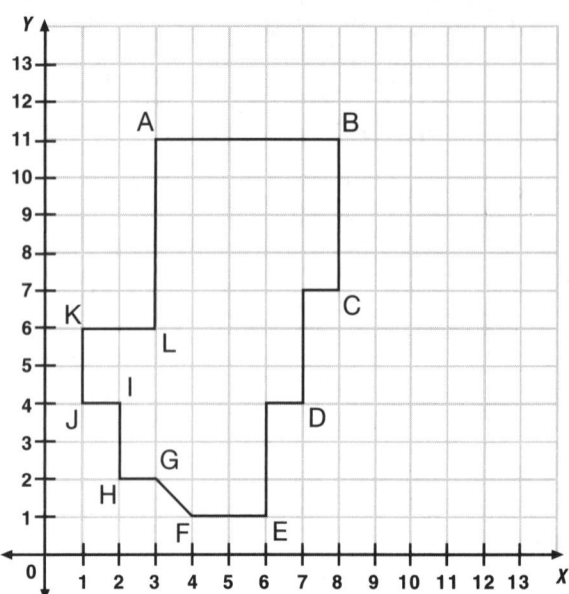

1. What is the ordered pair that represents B?
   - Ⓐ (3, 11)
   - Ⓑ (8, 11)
   - Ⓒ (3, 6)
   - Ⓓ (7, 4)

2. Which point is located at (3, 2)?
   - Ⓕ F
   - Ⓖ G
   - Ⓗ H
   - Ⓙ J

3. What is the ordered pair that represents L?
   - Ⓐ (3, 11)
   - Ⓑ (8, 11)
   - Ⓒ (3, 6)
   - Ⓓ (7, 4)

4. Which point is located at (2, 2)?
   - Ⓕ F
   - Ⓖ G
   - Ⓗ H
   - Ⓙ J

5. What is the ordered pair that represents A?
   - Ⓐ (3, 11)
   - Ⓑ (8, 11)
   - Ⓒ (3, 6)
   - Ⓓ (7, 4)

DIRECTIONS: Use the following graph for questions 6 and 7.

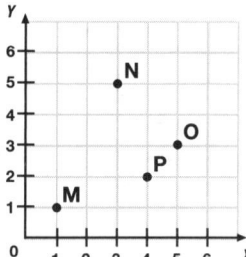

6. What point is at (5, 3)?
   - Ⓕ M
   - Ⓖ N
   - Ⓗ O
   - Ⓙ P

7. What are the coordinates of point P?
   - Ⓐ (4, 2)
   - Ⓑ (1, 1)
   - Ⓒ (3, 5)
   - Ⓓ (5, 3)

120

Name _____ Date _____

Mathematics
3.E **Graphing Ordered Number Pairs**

Function and Algebra Concepts

DIRECTIONS: Plot the following ordered pairs on the graph. Connect the points with line segments in the order given.

> Remember that points on a graph are labeled using ordered, or coordinate, pairs. The first value in the pair represents the horizontal distance from zero. A positive number means to move right. A negative number means to move left. The second value in the pair represents the vertical distance from zero. A positive number means to move up. A negative number means to move down.
>
> Look at the example point graphed on the grid below. This point is 5 units to the left of zero and 4 units above zero. Therefore, it would be labeled (−5, 4). The point (−5, 4) is called a **coordinate pair** or an **ordered pair**.

1. FLAG

F = (2,6)
L = (5,6)
A = (5,4)
G = (5,2)

Draw a line from A to F.

2. BOXD

B = (−2,2)
O = (1,2)
X = (1,−1)
D = (−2,−1)

Draw a line from D to B.

3. SHAPE

S = (2,−3)
H = (2,−5)
A = (−2,−5)
P = (−2,−6)
E = (−5,−6)

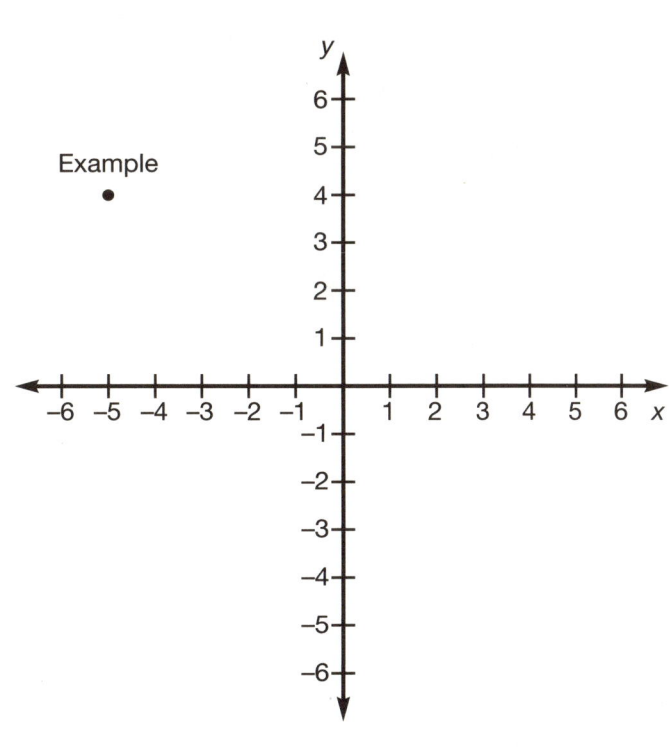

121

Name _____ Date _____

Mathematics
 3.F

Using Ordered Pairs to Construct Figures

Function and Algebra Concepts

DIRECTIONS: Plot the points to create four figures on the graph. Connect points with line segments in the order given (go down the columns).

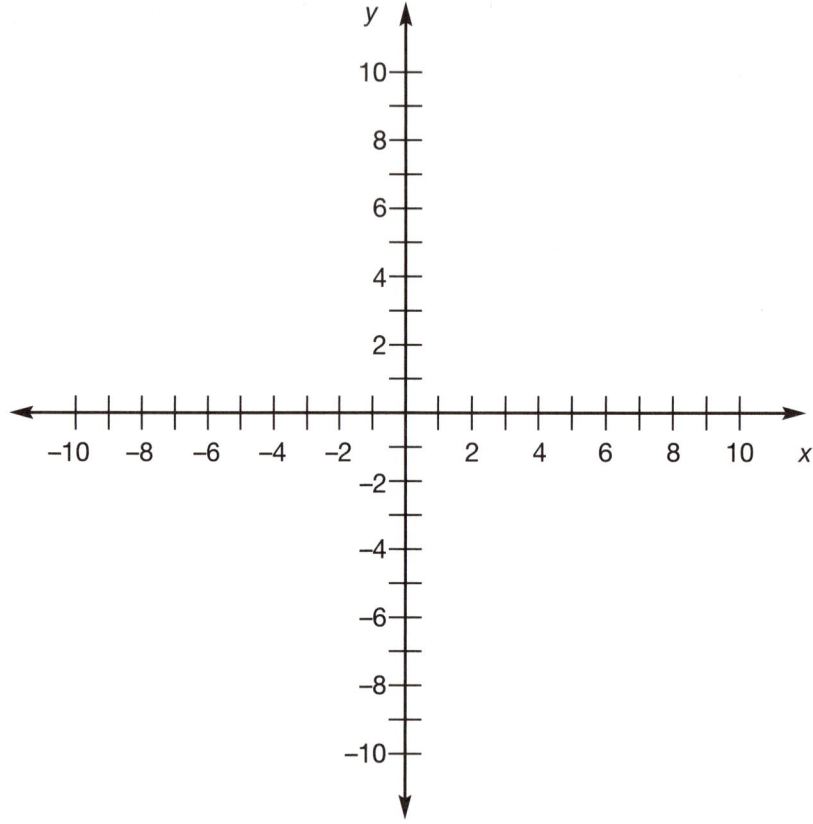

Figure 1	Figure 2	Figure 3	Figure 4
(–7, 1)	(7, 1)	(–7, –2)	(5, –5)
(–5, 1)	(7, 3)	(–7, –5)	(5, –4)
(–5, 3)	(5, 3)	(–6, –5)	(4, –4)
(–3, 3)	(5, 5)	(–6, –4)	(4, –3)
(–3, 1)	(7, 5)	(–5, –4)	(5, –3)
(–1, 1)	(7, 7)	(–5, –5)	(5, –2)
(–1, 7)	(1, 7)	(–4, –5)	(2, –2)
(–3, 7)	(1, 5)	(–4, –2)	(2, –3)
(–3, 5)	(3, 5)	(–5, –2)	(3, –3)
(–5, 5)	(3, 3)	(–5, –3)	(3, –4)
(–5, 7)	(1, 3)	(–6, –3)	(2, –4)
(–7, 7)	(1, 1)	(–6, –2)	(2, –5)
(–7, 1)	(7, 1)	(–7, –2)	(5, –5)

122

Name _____   Date _____

Mathematics
3.G

Understanding Functions

Function and Algebra Concepts

DIRECTIONS: Complete the table for each function rule given below.

1. **Rule:** $m = n + 3$

IN(n)	12	14	16	18	20	22
OUT(m)	15	17	19			

2. **Rule:** $m = 3n$

IN(n)	0	1	2	3	4	5
OUT(m)						

3. **Rule:** $m = 3n - 3$

IN(n)	2	4	6	8	10	12
OUT(m)						

DIRECTIONS: Find the function rule for each table below.

4.

IN(x)	6	7	9	11	14	16
OUT(y)	10	11	13	15	18	20

Rule: $y =$ _____

5.

IN(x)	1	3	6	8	10	13
OUT(y)	4	12	24	32	40	54

Rule: $y =$ _____

6.

IN(x)	10	13	16	19	22	25
OUT(y)	8	11	14	17	20	23

Rule: $y =$ _____

STOP

Name _____   Date _____

Mathematics

3.H Applying the Order of Operations

Function and Algebra Concepts

 **Clue** Look for key words, numbers, and figures in each problem, and be sure you perform the correct operation.

DIRECTIONS: Choose the best answer.

1. A desk normally costs $129. It is on sale for $99. How much would you save if you bought 2 desks on sale?
   - (A) ($129 + $99) × 2 = s
   - (B) ($129 − $99) ÷ 2 = s
   - (C) ($129 − $99) × 2 = s
   - (D) ($129 + $99) ÷ 2 = s

2. The highway department uses 6 gallons of paint for every 10 blocks of highway stripe. How many gallons will be needed for 250 blocks of highway stripe?
   - (F) (6 × 10) + 250 = g
   - (G) 250 − (10 ÷ 6) = g
   - (H) 250 × 10 × 6 = g
   - (J) (250 ÷ 10) × 6 = g

3. A hiker started out with 48 ounces of water. She drank 9 ounces of water after hiking 5 miles and 16 more when she reached mile marker 8. How many ounces of water did she have left?
   - (A) 48 − (9 + 16) = w
   - (B) 48 + (9 − 16) = w
   - (C) (16 − 9) + 48 = w
   - (D) 48 + (9 + 16) = w

4. Evaluate $(2a − 3b) + 4c$, if $a = 4$, $b = 3$, and $c = 2$.
   - (F) 25
   - (G) 38
   - (H) 7
   - (J) 12

5. Evaluate $5g + 2h$, if $g = 1$ and $h = 4$.
   - (A) 13
   - (B) 28
   - (C) 22
   - (D) 7

6. A barrel is 36 inches from top to bottom. The water in the barrel is $12\frac{1}{2}$ inches deep. How much space is there from the surface of the water to the top of the barrel?
   - (F) $s = 36 \div 12\frac{1}{2}$
   - (G) $s = 36 \times 12\frac{1}{2}$
   - (H) $s = 36 − 12\frac{1}{2}$
   - (J) $s = 36 + 12\frac{1}{2}$

7. The base of Sandy Mountain is 5,400 feet above sea level. The top of the mountain is 10,700 feet above sea level. A trail runs from the base of the mountain to the top. The trail is 8 miles long, and it takes about 5 hours to hike from the base of the mountain to the top. Which of the following equations could be used to determine the vertical distance from the base of the mountain to the top?
   - (A) $t − b = 5,300$
   - (B) $t + b = 16,100$
   - (C) $t \times b = 57,780,000$
   - (D) $t \div b = 1.98$

STOP

124

Name _____ Date _____

Mathematics

3.1

Equivalent Open Sentences

Function and Algebra Concepts

DIRECTIONS: Choose the best answer.

 A **solution set** is the answer that makes an open sentence true.

1. Which of the following open sentences has the same solution set as $21 - n = 10$?
   - (A) $n = 5 \times 2 - 1$
   - (B) $12 + n = 26$
   - (C) $30 - n = 21$
   - (D) $n = 10 + 1$

2. Which of the following open sentences have the same solution set?
   - (F) $6 + n = 18$; $20 - n = 18$
   - (G) $12 \div n = 27$; $n \div 3 = 6$
   - (H) $18 \div n = 3$; $4n = 24$
   - (J) $25 - n = 16$; $n + 8 = 16$

3. Which of the following open sentences have the same solution set?
   - (A) $6 + x = x + 5 + 1$
   - (B) $5(2 + x) = 5(2) - 5(x)$
   - (C) $6 + 2x = 6 + 2 + x$
   - (D) $9 - x = 9(x)$

4. Which of the following open sentences have the same solution set?
   - (F) $4 + y = 10 - y$
   - (G) $4(y + 2) = 4(y) + 8$
   - (H) $5 \times y = 2 \times 3 + y$
   - (J) $0 + y = 0y$

5. Which of the following open sentences has the same solution set as $4 + z = 16$?
   - (A) $z(2 + 2) = 36$
   - (B) $z(2) + 2 = 12$
   - (C) $z \times 2 - 5 = 19$
   - (D) $4 - 2 + z = 10$

6. Which of the following open sentences has the same solution set as $15 \times r = 75$?
   - (F) $4r = 20$
   - (G) $r + 15 = 18$
   - (H) $21 - r = 15$
   - (J) $36 \div r = 9$

7. Which of the following open sentences has the same solution set as $n + 12 = 35$?
   - (A) $46 \div n = 2$
   - (B) $n - 10 = 10$
   - (C) $n \times 3 = 45$
   - (D) $105 \div n = 5$

STOP

Name _____ Date _____

Mathematics

 3.J

Using Variables and Equal Symbols

Function and Algebra Concepts

Example:

Let $w = -2$, $y = 3$, and $z = \frac{1}{2}$

Then $w(2z - 4y) = -2(2 \times \frac{1}{2} - 4 \times 3)$
$= -2(1 - 12)$
$= -2 \times -11$
$= 22$

DIRECTIONS: Evaluate the following expressions if $w = \frac{1}{3}$, $y = 4$, and $z = -2$.

1. $3w =$ _____

2. $y + z =$ _____

3. $y - z =$ _____

4. $w(8 + y) =$ _____

5. $6zw =$ _____

6. $3(y + z) - 6w =$ _____

DIRECTIONS: Evaluate the following expressions if $a = -3$, $b = 8$, and $c = \frac{1}{2}$

7. $4a + 3b =$ _____

8. $(2a - b)c =$ _____

9. $2(a + b) - 10c =$ _____

10. $b[(12c - 3a)2 - 10] =$ _____

11. $(a - b)2c + b + 2a =$ _____

12. $(a + 2c)(b - 5) =$ _____

126

Name _____ Date _____

Mathematics

Identifying True Number Sentences

Function and Algebra Concepts

DIRECTIONS: On the blanks next to each number sentence, write **T** if the sentence is true and **F** if the sentence is false.

_____ 1. $8 + 4 = 6 \times 2$

_____ 2. $\frac{27}{9} = 0 \times 3$

_____ 3. $21 \times 3 = 60 + 3$

_____ 4. $12 \times 3 = 9 \times 4$

_____ 5. $8 + 7 = 14 \times 2$

_____ 6. $18 \times 2 = 9 \times 2 + 2$

_____ 7. $56 - y = (7 \times 8) - y$

_____ 8. $3 \times a = 3 - 1 \times a$

_____ 9. $16 + x = 10 + 6 + x$

_____ 10. $m + m = 2(m)$

_____ 11. $n + 6(3 - 1) = 15 + n$

_____ 12. $(y \times 8) + 5 = 23 - y$

_____ 13. $n^2 + 5 = 18 - n$

_____ 14. $25 - p = 15 + p$

_____ 15. $3y + 1 = 29 - y$

127

Name _____ Date _____

Mathematics 3.L

Writing True Number Sentences

Function and Algebra Concepts

DIRECTIONS: For each number sentence below, write <, >, or = in the box to make the sentence true.

1. 30 + 40 ☐ 50 + 21

2. $\frac{1}{2}$ × 50 ☐ 20 + 30

3. 42 × 2 ☐ 20 × 4

4. 3(4 + 2) ☐ 9 × 2

5. 71 − 45 ☐ 3 × 10

6. 49 ÷ 7 ☐ $\frac{40}{10}$

7. 54 × 2 ☐ 31 × 3

8. 75 ÷ 25 ☐ 60 ÷ 30

9. $\frac{2}{3} \times \frac{2}{4}$ ☐ $\frac{30}{90}$

10. 4(12 − 5) ☐ 5(10 − 5)

11. 62 − 50 ☐ 3(8 − 4)

12. 23 × 3 ☐ 15 × 4

13. 48 ÷ 6 ☐ 2 × 8

14. 4^2 + 5 ☐ 42 ÷ 2

15. 5(12 + 7) ☐ 12 × 8

16. 11 × 12 ☐ 4^3 × 2

Name _____ Date _____

Mathematics
3.M

Using Variables

Function and Algebra Concepts

DIRECTIONS: Read the following problems. Choose a variable for the unknown amount. Then, write a number sentence to represent the problem.

> **Example:**
>
> A **variable** is an amount that is not known. It is often represented by a letter. Variables are used in number sentences that represent a situation.
>
> Kyle made a dozen cookies. His little sister ate 5 of them. How many cookies are left?
>
> Variable: Let c = number of cookies left.
>
> Number Sentence: $c + 5 = 12$

1. You helped your mom plant 40 tulip bulbs in the fall. In the spring, 10 of the tulips did not come up at all, and $\frac{1}{3}$ of the rest had yellow flowers. Write a number sentence that shows how to find the number of tulips that had yellow flowers.

   _____

2. A train has 160 seats. Passengers are in 97 of them. Write an equation to find out how many seats are empty.

   _____

3. A VCR normally costs $119. It is on sale for $99. Write an equation to find out how much you would save if you bought 2 VCRs on sale.

   _____

4. Angelica is helping her dad build a deck. The surface of the deck will be 12 feet wide and 14 feet long. The boards they are using can cover an area of 4 square feet each. Write an equation that shows how many boards they will need to cover the surface of the deck.

   _____

5. Your uncle bought 375 feet of wire fencing. He put up 325 feet today and saved the rest for tomorrow. Write an equation that shows how many feet of fencing he has left.

   _____

6. A carpenter has 12 pieces of wood that are each 9 feet long. He has to cut 2 feet from each piece of wood because of water damage. Write an equation that shows how much good wood is left.

   _____

Name _____   Date _____

Mathematics

Solving Equations

Function and Algebra Concepts

DIRECTIONS: Choose the best answer.

1. What is the value of z in the equation $12 \times z = 144$?
   - (A) 8
   - (B) 12
   - (C) 122
   - (D) 11

2. What is the value of x if $54 \div x = 9$?
   - (F) 7
   - (G) 6
   - (H) 63
   - (J) 45

3. What is the value of r if $17 \times r = 68$?
   - (A) 51
   - (B) 4
   - (C) 85
   - (D) 6

4. What is the value of a in the equation $(7 \times a) - 9 = 54$?
   - (F) 8
   - (G) 7
   - (H) 5
   - (J) 9

5. If $z + 8 = 31$, then $z =$
   - (A) 39
   - (B) 23
   - (C) 22
   - (D) 4

6. If 27 students each brought in 6 cookies, which equation shows how many cookies they brought in all?
   - (F) $27 + 6 = c$
   - (G) $27 \times 6 = c$
   - (H) $27 - 6 = c$
   - (J) $27 \div 6 = c$

7. Which equation shows the total attendance at the Science Fair if 67 girls and 59 boys attended?
   - (A) $67 - 59 = a$
   - (B) $67 + 59 = a$
   - (C) $67 \div 59 = a$
   - (D) $67 \times 59 = a$

8. Sergio spent $3.80 on heavy-duty string for his project. He bought 20 feet of string. Which equation could you use to find out the price per foot of the string?
   - (F) $\$3.80 + 20 = s$
   - (G) $\$3.80 - 20 = s$
   - (H) $\$3.80 \times 20 = s$
   - (J) $\$3.80 \div 20 = s$

STOP

Name _____ Date _____

Mathematics

3.0

For pages 117–130

Mini-Test 3

Function and Algebra Concepts

DIRECTIONS: Fill in the blanks to complete the numerical sequence.

1. 21,484,375; 4,296,875; _____; 171,875; 34,375; 6,875; _____; 275; 55

2. _____; 151,263; 21,609; 3,087; 441; 63; ____

3. 60, 120, 180, _____, 300, _____

DIRECTIONS: Use the grid for questions 4 and 5.

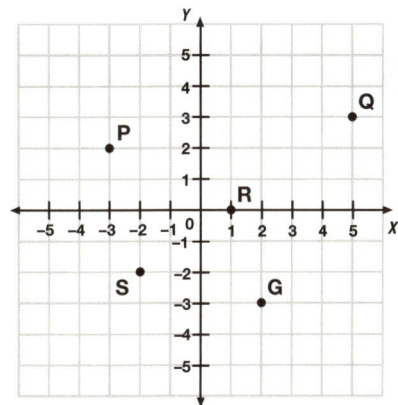

4. Which point is located at (5, 3)?
   - Ⓐ R
   - Ⓑ G
   - Ⓒ Q
   - Ⓓ P

5. What are the coordinates for point G?
   - Ⓕ (1, 1)
   - Ⓖ (2, −3)
   - Ⓗ (−2, −2)
   - Ⓙ (−3, 2)

DIRECTIONS: Choose the best answer.

6. Your mom planted a flower garden this spring. She planted 10 tulips, 8 daffodils, and 6 petunias in her garden. What fraction of the flowers are petunias?
   - Ⓐ $\frac{3}{4}$
   - Ⓑ $\frac{1}{4}$
   - Ⓒ $\frac{2}{3}$
   - Ⓓ $\frac{4}{5}$

7. Which of the following open sentences has the same solution set as $17 + x = 30$?
   - Ⓕ $x - 10 = 5$
   - Ⓖ $5x = 60$
   - Ⓗ $x + 33 = 45$
   - Ⓙ $78 \div x = 6$

8. Which one of the following number sentences is true?
   - Ⓐ $50 - 26 < 4 \times 7$
   - Ⓑ $2(3 + 5) = 4 \times 5$
   - Ⓒ $3(8 - 2) > 42 - 21$
   - Ⓓ $\frac{2}{3} \times 15 < \frac{1}{2} \times 16$

STOP

131

Mathematics Standards

4.0 Statistics and Probability Concepts
By the end of the school year, students should:

- **4.A** Collect, analyze, and interpret a variety of data. *(See page 133.)*
- **4.B** Construct and interpret double bar graphs, line graphs, circle graphs, histograms, and stem and leaf plots. *(See pages 134–136.)*
- **4.C** Compare various kinds of graphs to determine which best reflects the data. *(See page 137.)*
- **4.D** Use appropriate graphs to represent a variety of data. *(See page 138.)*
- **4.E** Use the average (mean), median, mode, and range to interpret and analyze data. *(See page 139.)*

What it means:
- The **mean** of a set of data is the sum of the data divided by the number of pieces of data (average).
- The **mode** of a set of data is the one that occurs most often.
- The **median** of a set of data is the number in the middle when the numbers are put in order.
- The **range** is the difference between the largest and smallest values.

- **4.F** Predict outcomes of probability experiments with independent events. *(See page 140.)*
- **4.G** Use simulation techniques to estimate probabilities. *(See pages 141–142.)*
- **4.H** Express probabilities as fractions, decimals, and percents. *(See page 143.)*
- **4.I** Understand and count the number of arrangements (permutations) or combinations that can be made from a set of objectives. *(See page 144.)*
- **4.J** Discover and use the multiplication principle (counting principle) through experiences with tree diagrams or lists of possible events taken in order. *(See pages 145–146.)*
- **4.K** Identify the sample space in a probability experiment. *(See page 146.)*

Name _____ Date _____

Mathematics
4.A

Analyzing Data

Statistics and Probability Concepts

DIRECTIONS: The sixth-grade class at M. L. King, Jr. Middle School collects items to donate to a local homeless shelter. The chart below shows an inventory of the items collected.

Items	Last Year	This Year
snack foods	21	32
paper goods	28	42
instant foods	22	38
canned goods	42	63
infant clothing	42	40

1. Find the mean number of items collected each year.
   Last Year: _____ This Year: _____

2. What was the difference in the mean number of items collected? _____

3. Which item showed the greatest increase from last year to this year? _____
   Which items showed a decrease? _____

4. Which year showed the most variation in the types of items collected? Explain.

   _____
   _____
   _____
   _____
   _____

133

Mathematics
4.B

Using Bar Graphs

Statistics and Probability Concepts

DIRECTIONS: Gina asked 250 students about their favorite types of restaurants. Her results are shown in the chart below.

Restaurant Type	Number
Italian	85
Bar & Grill	32
Mexican	45
Fast Food	70
Chinese	18

1. Each tick mark on the vertical axis should represent _____ people. Put a scale on the vertical axis.

2. Label the vertical axis.

3. What is the range of the data? _____

4. Complete the bar graph, using the data from the table.

Restaurant Preferences

Italian　　Bar & Grill　　Mexican　　Fast Food　　Chinese

134

Name _____ Date _____

Mathematics
4.B

Using Circle Graphs

Statistics and Probability Concepts

DIRECTIONS: The charts below represent surveys of students' favorites. Show the information from each chart in the circle graphs.

Example:

Circle graphs are best used to display parts of a whole. Below are the results from a survey about students' favorite school subject.

Subject	Percentage
English	20%
Math	10%
Science	10%
Social Studies	10%
Computers	20%
Music	30%

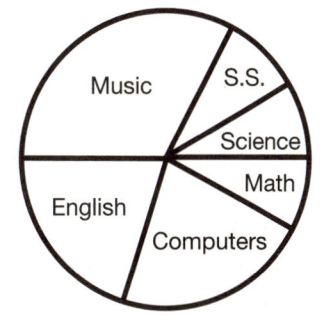

Ice-Cream Flavor	Percentage
Vanilla	10%
Chocolate	60%
Swirl	30%

Candy	Percentage
Chocolate	30%
Butterscotch	5%
Sour Balls	10%
Licorice	20%
Jelly Beans	10%
Suckers	25%

Types of Movies	Percentage
Animated	15%
Comedy	20%
Action	25%
Drama	10%
Horror	30%

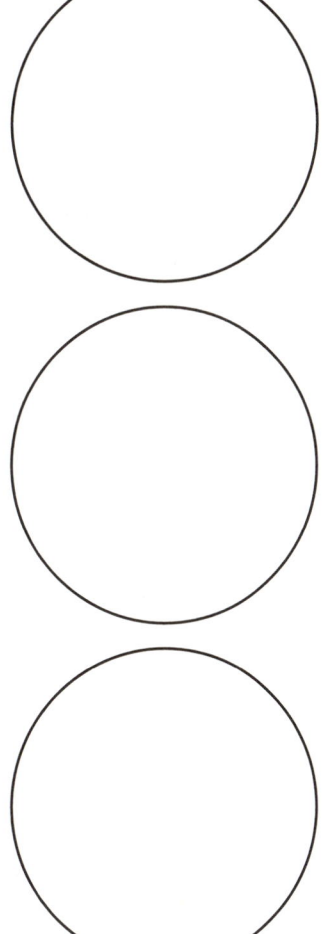

135

Name _____ Date _____

Mathematics

Using Stem and Leaf Plots

Statistics and Probability Concepts

DIRECTIONS: Make a stem and leaf plot for the following data. Ms. Jensen's class completed a math test. The test scores out of 50 possible points were: 49, 35, 37, 47, 43, 50, 44, 45, 48, 38, 41, 50, 45, 50.

Example:

To use a stem and leaf plot, each value in the data is split into a "stem" and a "leaf." The "leaf" is most often the last digit of the number. The other digits to the left of the "leaf" are the "stem." For example, in the number 214, the "stem" would be 21 and the "leaf" would be 4. You can show this in a table, such as this:

Stem	Leaf
21	4

The legend for the table would be: Legend: 21 | 4 means 214. If you have multiple entries, the leaves for each stem go in the same row. For example, the data 214, 216, 223, 217, and 224 would be shown this way in a table:

Stem	Leaf
21	4, 6, 7
22	3, 4

Math Test Scores (out of 50 points)

Stem	Leaf

Legend: 3 | 5 means 35

To find the median in a stem and leaf plot, count off half the total number of leaves.

What is the median grade for the math test? _____

136

Name _____ Date _____

Mathematics 4.C — Comparing Line and Bar Graphs
Statistics and Probability Concepts

DIRECTIONS: The data below shows a person's heart rate while jogging. Use the data to make both a line graph and a bar graph.

Data	
Time	Heart Rate
0 min.	80
5 min.	120
10 min.	135
15 min.	147
20 min.	159
25 min.	150

1. **Line Graph**
   Heart Rate While Jogging

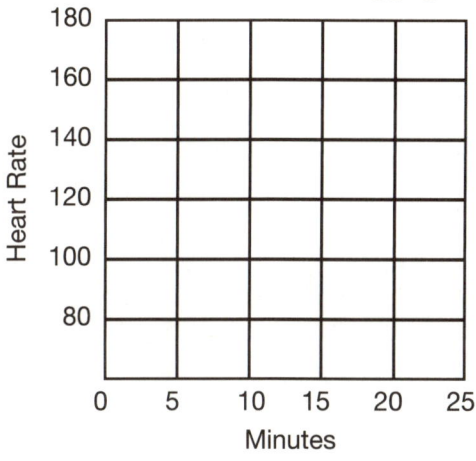

2. **Bar Graph**
   Heart Rate While Jogging

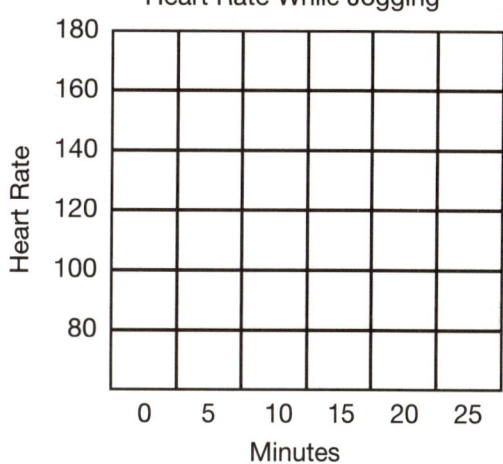

DIRECTIONS: Use the graphs to answer the following questions.

3. At what time was the jogger's heart rate the highest? _____

4. During which interval did the jogger's heart rate increase the most?

   _____

5. During which interval did the jogger's heart rate increase the least?

   _____

6. Which graph more clearly shows the changes in heart rate? Why?

   _____

Name _____   Date _____

Mathematics
4.D   # Using Appropriate Graphs

Statistics and Probability Concepts

DIRECTIONS: The school drama club hopes to raise enough money to buy costumes for their first play. Each of the 10 members was given 15 tins of popcorn and 15 bags of pretzels to sell. The bar graph below shows the results of the sale.

Member	Popcorn	Pretzels
Amelia		
Bobby		
Carla		
Daniel		
Elizabeth		
Frank		
Gerry		
Hank		
Isabella		
Jim		

1. Use the bar graph to complete the data table above.

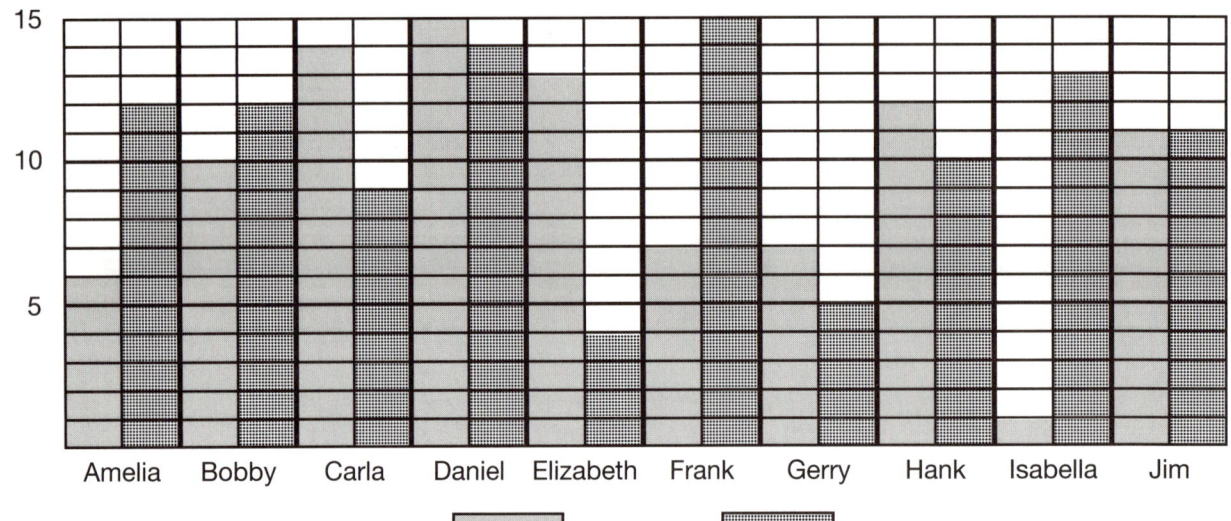

2. Who sold the most popcorn? _____
   The most pretzels? _____

3. Which sold best, the tins of popcorn or the bags of pretzels? _____

4. Who made the most total sales? _____
   The least total sales? _____

5. Which is a better way of showing this data—the table or the double bar graph? Explain why.

_____
_____
_____
_____

138

Name _____   Date _____

Mathematics
4.E **Mean, Median, Mode, and Range**   Statistics and Probability Concepts

---

DIRECTIONS: For each store, calculate the mean, median, mode, and range of prices for soccer cleats. All prices have been rounded to the nearest dollar.

Mean: average number
Median: middle number of ordered data
Mode: the value that occurs most often
Range: the difference between the largest and smallest values

1. Store 1 Prices

$45 $32
$45 $70 $45
$20 $48 $55
$50 $32

Mean: _____
Median: _____
Mode: _____
Range: _____

2. Store 2 Prices

$35 $40
$35 $25 $75
$50 $63 $80
$42 $35

Mean: _____
Median: _____
Mode: _____
Range: _____

3. Store 3 Prices

$85 $50 $45
$60 $45 $80
$85 $20 $85
$50 $100

Mean: _____
Median: _____
Mode: _____
Range: _____

4. Store 4 Prices

$55 $60
$88 $60 $32
$80 $48 $64
$80 $60

Mean: _____
Median: _____
Mode: _____
Range: _____

DIRECTIONS: Answer the following questions on another sheet of paper. Write your answers in complete sentences.

5. Store 3 claims they have shoes to fit any budget, since they have the largest range of prices. Look at the data for Store 3. Do you agree they have the best variety of prices? Explain.

6. Which store has the lowest average price?

7. If you wanted to find the store with the best variety of low-priced shoes, which would you choose? Which "middle number" could help you make this decision?

139

Name _____ Date _____

Mathematics

Independent and Dependent Events

Statistics and Probability Concepts

DIRECTIONS: Choose the best answer.

Example:

Flipping two coins is an example of _____ .

- Ⓐ independent events
- Ⓑ dependent events

Answer: Ⓐ

1. Pulling a card out of a stack and pulling a second card without replacing the first is an example of _____ .
   - Ⓐ independent events
   - Ⓑ dependent events

2. Picking teams for basketball is an example of _____ .
   - Ⓕ independent events
   - Ⓖ dependent events

3. Pulling socks out of a drawer is an example of _____ .
   - Ⓐ independent events
   - Ⓑ dependent events

4. A spinner has 4 equal sectors colored yellow, blue, green, and red. After spinning the spinner, you land on red. Spinning again and landing on green is an example of _____ .
   - Ⓕ independent events
   - Ⓖ dependent events

5. A 6-sided die is rolled. You roll an even number. Rolling again and getting an odd number is an example of _____ .
   - Ⓐ independent events
   - Ⓑ dependent events

DIRECTIONS: A bag of jellybeans contains 5 cherry jellybeans, 3 licorice jellybeans, 6 lime jellybeans, and 6 lemon jellybeans.

6. Carol wants a cherry jellybean. Without looking, she reaches into the bag and grabs a lime jellybean. She puts the jellybean back in the bag. Again, she randomly chooses a jellybean. This is an example of _____ .
   - Ⓕ independent events
   - Ⓖ dependent events

7. Malcolm likes only the licorice jellybeans. He randomly grabs a jellybean out of the bag. If it is not licorice, he gives it to a friend. Give the probability of getting a licorice jellybean *after* each of the grabs below.

   Probability of Licorice

   Grab 1: cherry _____
   Grab 2: lime   _____
   Grab 3: cherry _____
   Grab 4: lemon   _____
   Grab 5: lemon   _____

8. What happens to his chance of getting a licorice jellybean after each grab?

   _____

9. If Malcolm pulls out a licorice jellybean on his sixth grab, what is the chance he will get a licorice jellybean on the seventh grab?

   _____

140

Probability With Dice

Mathematics 4.G — Statistics and Probability Concepts

Probability: $\dfrac{\text{\# of ways the outcome could happen}}{\text{\# of total possibilities}}$

Find the probability of rolling a sum of 3 with two dice.

Probability = $\dfrac{2}{36} = \dfrac{1}{18}$

Ways to roll a 3:   or

\# total dice combinations: 36

DIRECTIONS: Think about rolling two six-sided dice. Which sum(s) are you most likely to roll? Least likely to roll? Complete the following activity to find out. Fill in the dice probability chart on the next page by following these directions.

First, draw in all possible combinations of dice pairs that will make each sum. Some of the sums are done for you.

Next, count the number of different ways you found the sum. Write this number in the "# of ways" column. You should find a total of 36 different pair combinations.

DIRECTIONS: Once you have completed the chart, answer the following questions.

1. Which sum is most likely to occur? _____

2. Which sums are least likely to occur? _____

3. Which sums have a $\dfrac{5}{36}$ chance of happening (meaning there are 5 possible ways to make the sum out of 36 total combinations)? _____

4. What is the probability of rolling a sum of 9? _____

5. What is the probability of rolling a sum of 10 or a sum of 5? _____

6. In many games, rolling doubles allows you to take another turn. How many different ways can you roll doubles? _____ What is the probability of rolling doubles? _____

GO →

Name _____   Date _____

Sum	Ways to make the sum	# of ways
2	⚀/⚀	1
3	⚀/⚁ ⚁/⚀	2
4	⚀/⚂ ⚁/⚁ ⚂/⚀	3
5		
6		
7	⚀/⚅ ⚅/⚀ ⚁/⚄ ⚄/⚁ ⚂/⚃ ⚃/⚂	6
8		
9		
10		
11		
12		
Total		36

142

Name _____   Date _____

Mathematics
4.H

Expressing Probability

Statistics and Probability Concepts

DIRECTIONS: Choose the best answer.

For questions 1–4, suppose you wrote the word VACATION on a strip of paper and cut the paper into pieces with one letter per piece. If you put the pieces into a hat and pulled out one piece without looking, determine the probability of each situation.

1. What is the probability that you would pick out the letter A?
   - Ⓐ 1 out of 8
   - Ⓑ 2 out of 8
   - Ⓒ 4 out of 5
   - Ⓓ 2 out of 7

2. Without returning the A to the hat, what is the probability that you would pick out the letter C?
   - Ⓕ 1 out of 8
   - Ⓖ 1 out of 7
   - Ⓗ 2 out of 8
   - Ⓙ 1 out of 6

3. Without returning the A or the C to the hat, what is the probability of picking a vowel?
   - Ⓐ 4 out of 8
   - Ⓑ 3 out of 7
   - Ⓒ 3 out of 5
   - Ⓓ 3 out of 6

4. Given the original word, what is the probability of picking a consonant?
   - Ⓕ 1 out of 8
   - Ⓖ 4 out of 8
   - Ⓗ 2 out of 8
   - Ⓙ 4 out of 6

There are ten white tennis balls and ten green tennis balls in a box. Tony reaches into the box without looking.

5. What is the probability that he will pick a white ball?
   - Ⓐ 10%
   - Ⓑ 50%
   - Ⓒ 5%
   - Ⓓ 20%

6. What is the probability that he will pick a green ball?
   - Ⓕ 0.10
   - Ⓖ 0.20
   - Ⓗ 0.05
   - Ⓙ 0.50

7. Tony picks a white ball. He returns it to the box. He wants another white ball. What is the probability that he will pick a white ball from the box on the next try?
   - Ⓐ $\frac{9}{16}$
   - Ⓑ $\frac{1}{19}$
   - Ⓒ $\frac{1}{5}$
   - Ⓓ $\frac{1}{2}$

Name _____ Date _____

Mathematics
4.1

Understanding Permutations

Statistics and Probability Concepts

DIRECTIONS: Use the sample below to determine the number of arrangements that can be made from the following situations. Show your work below.

> **Example:**
>
> A permutation is an arrangement of a group of things in a certain order. It is a way of figuring out how many different ways a group of objects can be arranged. For example, imagine that a family of five wants to be seated in a row of chairs for a picture. How many ways can that family be seated?
>
> First, make five blanks: ___ ___ ___ ___ ___
>
> There are five choices for the first blank, because any of the five people can be seated in the first chair.
>
>   _5_ ___ ___ ___ ___
>
> In the second chair, there are only 4 choices left, because one of the people has been chosen for the first chair.
>
>   _5_ _4_ ___ ___ ___
>
> Then, there are 3 choices left, then 2, then 1. So, the answer is $5 \times 4 \times 3 \times 2 \times 1 = 120$. There are 120 different ways that the family members can be arranged in a row to take a picture.

1. How many different ways can 6 students stand in a single file waiting to go to lunch?

2. A petition is being sent around your neighborhood to get a community pool. How many different ways can 10 people sign their names in the blank lines on the petition?

Name _____   Date _____

Mathematics

Using the Counting Principle

Statistics and Probability Concepts

DIRECTIONS: Answer the following questions using the counting principle.

> **Example:**
>
> When you are dealing with more than one event, you can determine the number of possible outcomes that exist. You can do this by using the counting principle. In this principle, you multiply each stage or event by the number of choices. For example, say you are getting dressed to go outside. You can choose from 2 coats, 3 hats, and 4 pairs of gloves. There are 3 stages or events: 2 choices for the coat, 3 choices for the hat, and 4 choices for the gloves. To figure out the number of combinations, multiply:
>
> | Coats | | Hats | | Gloves | | # of Combinations |
> |---|---|---|---|---|---|---|
> | 2 | × | 3 | × | 4 | = | 24 |

1. You toss a quarter 4 times. How many arrangements of heads and tails are possible?

   Toss 1   ×   Toss 2   ×   Toss 3   ×   Toss 4   =   # of arrangements

   _____   _____   _____   _____   _____

2. You are at a movie theater with your dad, and he tells you that you can have one drink, one kind of candy, and one size of popcorn. The movie theater sells 3 sizes of drink, 6 kinds of candy, and 3 sizes of popcorn. How many combinations of drink, candy, and popcorn can you make?

   Drink   ×   Candy   ×   Popcorn   =   # of combinations

   _____   _____   _____   _____

3. A store sells girls' inline skates in 5 different colors; in sizes 4, 5, 6, 7, and 8; and with tassels, striped laces, or bells. How many possible arrangements of inline skates can be purchased?

   Colors   ×   Sizes   ×   Adornment   =   # of arrangements

   _____   _____   _____   _____

145

Name _____   Date _____

Mathematics

Identifying Sample Spaces

Statistics and Probability Concepts

DIRECTIONS: Choose the best answer.

> **Clue**   A **sample space** is a set of all possible outcomes for an activity.

1. There are 10 silver earrings and 10 gold earrings in a drawer. Cheryl reaches into her jewelry box without looking. What is the probability that she will pick a gold earring?

   - (A) $\frac{1}{2}$
   - (B) $\frac{1}{3}$
   - (C) $\frac{1}{4}$
   - (D) None of the above

2. A group of teachers are ordering sandwiches from the deli. They can choose ham, beef, turkey, or bologna on white bread, wheat bread, or rye bread. How many different meat and bread combinations are possible?

   - (F) 12
   - (G) 16
   - (H) 7
   - (J) None of the above

3. Elliott spun the arrow on a spinner 30 times. The results are shown in the table. Which of these spinners did Elliott most likely spin?

Diamond	Heart	Spade	Total Spins
11	10	9	30

     (A)   (B)   (C)   (D)

4. A snack food company makes chewy fruit shapes of lions, monkeys, elephants, and giraffes in red, green, purple, and yellow. They put the same number of each kind in a package. How many different outcomes are there?

   - (F) 4
   - (G) 8
   - (H) 16
   - (J) None of the above

DIRECTIONS: For questions 5 and 6, draw a tree diagram to show all the outcomes.

5. Draw the tree diagram for question 2.

6. A new car can be ordered in black, red, or tan. You may also choose leather or fabric seats. Show the outcomes.

Name _____   Date _____

Mathematics

4.0

For pages 133–146

Mini-Test 4

Statistics and Probability Concepts

DIRECTIONS: Mr. Vandersy's class earned $582.00 during the school year in order to purchase new books for the library. The graph below shows the percentage of money earned from each activity. Use it to answer questions 1 and 2.

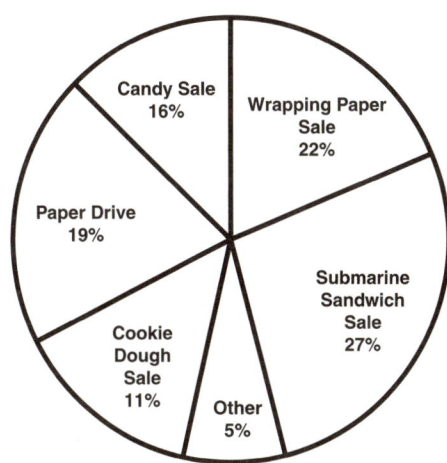

1. Which fund-raiser earned the most money?
   - (A) the candy sale
   - (B) the wrapping paper sale
   - (C) the submarine sandwich sale
   - (D) the paper drive

2. How much money was earned from the cookie dough sale?
   - (F) $63.02
   - (G) $123.02
   - (H) $64.02
   - (J) $73.03

DIRECTIONS: Use the data set for questions 3–5. The test scores for a class are: 86, 94, 70, 81, 92, 74, 75, 89, 76, 97.

3. What is the mean of the data?
   - (A) 27
   - (B) 83.4
   - (C) 83.5
   - (D) None of the above

4. What is the median of the data?
   - (F) 27
   - (G) 83.4
   - (H) 83.5
   - (J) None of the above

5. Create a stem and leaf plot using the data set.

Stem	Leaf

DIRECTIONS: Choose the best answer.

6. The sweaters on sale come in three styles: pullover, cardigan, and turtleneck. They come in three colors: black, white, and red. How many choices are there?
   - (A) 9
   - (B) 6
   - (C) 3
   - (D) 12

7. For question 6, what is the probability of choosing a black pullover?
   - (F) $\frac{1}{12}$
   - (H) $\frac{1}{6}$
   - (G) $\frac{1}{9}$
   - (J) $\frac{1}{3}$

8. A coin is tossed, and a single 6-sided die is rolled. The probability of getting a head on the coin and a 3 on the die is an example of _____.
   - (A) independent events
   - (B) dependent events

STOP

Mathematics Standards

5.0 Mathematical Process
By the end of the school year, students should:
- **5.A** Create, analyze, and solve word problems in all of the concept areas. *(See page 149.)*
- **5.B** Identify pertinent, extraneous, and missing information. *(See pages 150–151.)*
- **5.C** Use a variety of strategies to solve and represent problems and solutions (e.g., logical thinking, estimation, number sense, pictures, diagrams, and charts). *(See page 152.)*
- **5.D** Work individually and collaboratively to discuss, justify, organize, and write about solutions to problems using content-specific mathematical language.
- **5.E** Apply basic math skills to real-world situations. *(See page 153.)*
- **5.F** Explore the use of appropriate mathematical tools and technology (e.g., computers, basic scientific calculators, protractors, compasses, scales, and rulers—metric and U.S. Standard).

Name _____ Date _____

Mathematics

Solving Word Problems

Mathematical Process

DIRECTIONS: Choose the best answer.

1. Computer headphones cost $13.95. Ms. Jackson wants to buy 24 pairs of headphones for the school computer lab. How much will it cost altogether to buy the headphones?
   - (A) $335.90
   - (B) $334.80
   - (C) $324.80
   - (D) None of the above

2. There are 2,464 monkeys in a nature preserve. They live in groups of 16. How many groups of monkeys are there?
   - (F) 154 groups
   - (G) 164 groups
   - (H) 153 groups
   - (J) None of the above

3. Mason, Clare, and Clark each bought candy in the bulk food store. The candy they bought weighed 2 pounds, 4 pounds, and 3 pounds. How many pounds of candy did they buy in all?
   - (A) $12\frac{11}{12}$
   - (B) $11\frac{1}{24}$
   - (C) $10\frac{11}{24}$
   - (D) None of the above

4. A shoebox is 6 inches wide, 11 inches long, and 5 inches high. What is the volume of the box?
   - (F) 330 cubic inches
   - (G) 22 cubic inches
   - (H) 230 cubic inches
   - (J) None of the above

5. Connie earned $6.00 by baby-sitting. She added that money to some allowance she had saved and bought a new video game for $22.79. She had $2.88 left over. How much allowance had Connie saved?
   - (A) $19.91
   - (B) $13.78
   - (C) $19.67
   - (D) $18.77

6. How much change will you receive from $2.00 if you buy a pencil for $0.19 and a pen for $0.79?
   - (F) $1.21
   - (G) $1.81
   - (H) $1.01
   - (J) $1.02

7. Todd traveled 1,378 miles from Florida to Connecticut. Melanie traveled 3,095 miles from California to Connecticut. How many more miles did Melanie have to travel than Todd?
   - (A) 1,717 miles
   - (B) 2,717 miles
   - (C) 1,727 miles
   - (D) 1,617 miles

8. How much change will you receive from $5.00 if you buy a shake for $1.29, a hamburger for $0.99, and fries for $0.89?
   - (F) $1.82
   - (G) $1.83
   - (H) $3.71
   - (J) $2.83

STOP

Mathematics 5.B: Identifying Necessary Information

Mathematical Process

DIRECTIONS: Choose the best answer.

1. Jeremy opened a savings account. He deposited $23.45 into his account. The monthly rate of interest on his account is 5%. How much interest would Jeremy receive on that amount at the end of the month?
   - A) $1.17
   - B) $117.25
   - C) $17.25
   - D) $0.17

2. It takes 4 workers about 18 hours to build a garage. How long would it take to build a garage if there were 12 workers?
   - F) 54 hours
   - G) 6 hours
   - H) 3 hours
   - J) None of the above

3. Suppose you knew the monthly cost of cable television, the number of channels you can receive, and the number of people in a family. Which of these questions could you answer?
   - A) the amount of time spent watching TV
   - B) the average cost per channel
   - C) how long it takes to install the cable
   - D) the average cost per program

DIRECTIONS: Read this passage, then answer questions 4–6.

A bus driver began her route with an empty bus. She picked up 8 passengers at the first stop. Each passenger paid $1.50. At the next stop, 12 passengers got on. Half of them were senior citizens, so they paid only $0.75. At the third stop, 5 more passengers got on the bus and 8 got off.

4. What was the total number of passengers that got on the bus?
   - F) 17
   - G) 25
   - H) 19
   - J) 33

5. What was the total amount of money the passengers paid?
   - A) $37.50
   - B) $27.50
   - C) $33.00
   - D) $33.50

6. After the third stop, how many people were on the bus?
   - F) 33
   - G) 19
   - H) 18
   - J) 17

GO

Name _____   Date _____

DIRECTIONS: Choose the best answer.

7. Nine people go for a ride in two cars. One car holds three more people than the other. How many men are in each car?

    (A) 2 in one car and 3 in another
    (B) 1 in one car and 4 in another
    (C) 3 in one car and 1 in another
    (D) not enough information

8. An electrician has 300 feet of wire. He uses 275 feet and saves the rest for another job. How many feet of wire does he have left?

    (F) 300 + ■ = 275
    (G) 300 + 275 = ■
    (H) 300 − 275 = ■
    (J) ■ = 300 + 275

9. When Sandy and her father went to the supermarket, they bought $17.84 worth of food. Sandy's father paid for the food with a $20 bill. Which of these is the correct amount of change they should receive?

    (A) 2 one-dollar bills, 1 dime, 1 nickel, and 1 penny
    (B) 3 one-dollar bills, 1 dime, 1 nickel, and 1 penny
    (C) 2 one-dollar bills, 1 dime, 2 nickels, and 1 penny
    (D) 2 one-dollar bills, 1 dime, 3 nickels, and 1 penny

10. Suppose you knew the number of pages in a book, how long it takes to read a page, and the number of words on a page. Which of these questions could you *not* answer?

    (F) How many letters are in the book?
    (G) How long does it take to read the book?
    (H) How many words are in the book?
    (J) How long does it take to read the number of words on one page?

DIRECTIONS: Read this passage, then answer questions 11 and 12.

Harriet and Bernardo volunteered to pick up litter at a park near their home. They will work from 9:00 A.M. to 2:00 P.M. each Saturday.

11. If there are 4 Saturdays in a month, how many hours in all do Harriet and Bernardo work in a month?

    (A) 35 hours
    (B) 5 hours
    (C) 24 hours
    (D) 40 hours

12. It usually takes one person 2 hours to fill one bag of trash at the park. How many bags of trash will Harriet and Bernardo pick up together in one day?

    (F) 4
    (G) 2.5
    (H) 5
    (J) 3

Name _____ Date _____

Mathematics

5.C

Using Strategies to Solve Problems

Mathematical Process

DIRECTIONS: Choose the best answer.

1. What number completes this number sentence?

   4 × 35 = 4 × (■ + 5)

   - Ⓐ 35
   - Ⓑ 30
   - Ⓒ 3
   - Ⓓ 38

2. Lizette makes cubes from blocks to display kitchen gadgets and cookware in her store as shown below. How many blocks will she use to make Display 6?

   Display 1   Display 2   Display 3

   - Ⓕ 36
   - Ⓖ 64
   - Ⓗ 125
   - Ⓙ 216

3. Thirteen people ride to school in 2 cars. One car holds three more people than the other. How many people are in each car?

   - Ⓐ 8 in one car and 5 in the other
   - Ⓑ 9 in one car and 4 in the other
   - Ⓒ 7 in one car and 6 in the other
   - Ⓓ 3 in one car and 10 in the other

4. How many more glass balls are needed to fill the box to the top?

   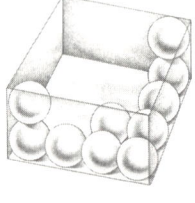

   - Ⓕ 20
   - Ⓖ 22
   - Ⓗ 24
   - Ⓙ 26

5. About how much will the popcorn on the scale cost?

   58¢ a pound   68¢ a pound   78¢ a pound   98¢ a pound $1.18 a pound

   - Ⓐ $1.80
   - Ⓑ $2.50
   - Ⓒ $3.25
   - Ⓓ $4.95

6. Nako is using nickels to measure the area of a dollar bill. About how many nickels will it take to cover the dollar bill?

   - Ⓕ about 50
   - Ⓖ about 21
   - Ⓗ about 18
   - Ⓙ about 10

7. Which of these statements is correct?

   - Ⓐ 9 quarters is worth more than 12 dimes.
   - Ⓑ 12 dimes is worth more than 50 nickels.
   - Ⓒ 50 nickels is worth less than 9 quarters.
   - Ⓓ 50 nickels is worth less than 12 dimes.

8. What is the perimeter of this rectangle?

   - Ⓕ 33 cm
   - Ⓖ 60 cm
   - Ⓗ 66 cm
   - Ⓙ 68 cm

   6 cm
   27 cm

   STOP

Name _____ Date _____

Mathematics
5.E

Applying Math to Real-World Situations

Mathematical Process

DIRECTIONS: Choose the best answer.

1. School begins at 8:45 A.M. The sixth graders eat lunch 2 hours and 45 minutes later. Lunch lasts 30 minutes. Which clock shows the time the sixth graders return to class after eating lunch?

   Ⓐ

   Ⓑ

   Ⓒ

   Ⓓ

2. Each member of Wanda's family had one hamburger for lunch. Each hamburger costs $4.95. What else do you need to know to find out how much the family spent on lunch?

   Ⓕ which family member paid for lunch
   Ⓖ how many people are in the family
   Ⓗ the price of hot dogs
   Ⓙ how much money Wanda's father had in his wallet

3. Sally and Susie together have more money in their piggy banks than Tom has in his. If Tom has $35.00 and Susie has $17.00, then Sally must have _____ .

   Ⓐ less than $17.00
   Ⓑ exactly $18.00
   Ⓒ between $17.00 and $18.00
   Ⓓ more than $18.00

4. Arnie wants to serve each of his friends a donut and a can of apple juice. There are 8 donuts in a pack, but only 6 cans of juice in a pack. What is the fewest number of donuts and cans of juice that Arnie must buy so that he has the same number of each?

   Ⓕ 6
   Ⓖ 8
   Ⓗ 16
   Ⓙ 24

5. Steven went grocery shopping with his mother. The groceries totaled $36.37. Steven's mom paid for the food with two $20 bills. Which of these is the correct amount of change she should receive?

   Ⓐ 2 one-dollar bills, two quarters, two dimes, and three pennies
   Ⓑ 3 one-dollar bills, two quarters, one dime, and three pennies
   Ⓒ 3 one-dollar bills, three quarters, one nickel, and three pennies
   Ⓓ None of the above

STOP

Name _____   Date _____

Mathematics

5.0

For pages 149–153

Mini-Test 5

Mathematical Process

DIRECTIONS: Choose the best answer.

1. The Mathematics Building is 68.3 feet from the Computer Center. The Library is 5 times farther from the Computer Center than the Mathematics Building. What is the distance from the Computer Center to the Library?

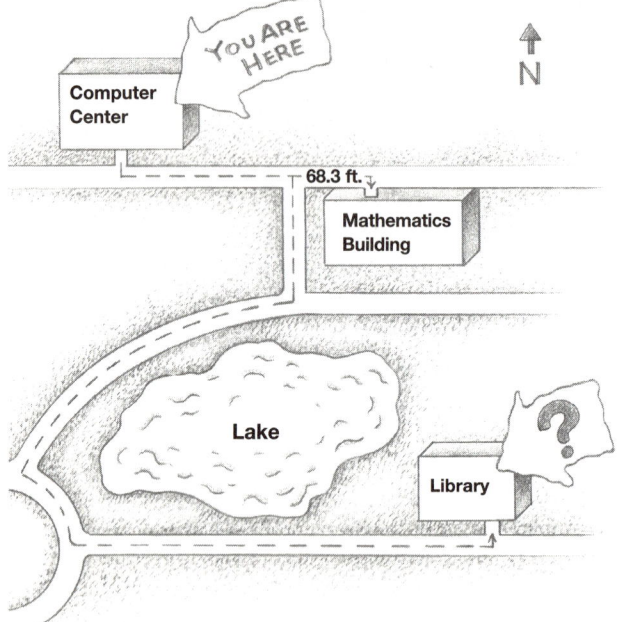

- (A) 3415.0 feet
- (B) 341.5 feet
- (C) 73.3 feet
- (D) 13.66 feet

2. The supermarket in the town of Garret has 18 full-time workers and 7 part-time workers. How many more full-time workers are there than part-time workers?

- (F) 25
- (G) 19
- (H) 12
- (J) 11

3. Diane has been hired by the supermarket as a part-time worker. She will earn $5.50 an hour, and she hopes to work 12 hours each week. How much will she earn in a week?

- (A) $66.00
- (B) $56.50
- (C) $17.50
- (D) $60.50

4. If Diane stays on the job for 6 months, she will receive a $0.50 an hour raise. If she stays 6 more months, she will receive another raise of $0.75. How much will Diane earn if she stays on the job for 12 more months?

- (F) $1.25
- (G) $6.00
- (H) $6.75
- (J) None of the above

5. Jessica has been collecting baseball cards since she was in second grade. She has them in notebooks in card protectors. Each notebook has 100 pages, and each page holds 9 cards. If she has 2 full notebooks and 1 that is half full, how many cards does she have in all?

- (A) 900
- (B) 1,800
- (C) 2,250
- (D) 2,400

6. Lisa bought a used car that cost $4,000. She had to pay $1,000 down, which left a balance of $3,000. She paid $75 a month until she had paid the entire amount. How many months did she make payments?

- (F) 45
- (G) 40
- (H) 35
- (J) 30

STOP

154

How Am I Doing?

Mini-Test 1

Pages 91–92

Number Correct

16–20 answers correct	**Great Job!** Move on to the section test on page 157.
11–15 answers correct	**You're almost there!** But you still need a little practice. Review the practice pages 66–90 before moving on to the section test on page 157.
0–10 answers correct	**Oops!** Time to review what you have learned and try again. Review the practice section on pages 66–90. Then, retake the test on page 91–92. Now, move on to the section test on page 157.

Mini-Test 2

Pages 114–115

Number Correct

14–17 answers correct	**Awesome!** Move on to the section test on page 157.
10–13 answers correct	**You're almost there!** But you still need a little practice. Review the practice pages 94–113 before moving on to the section test on page 157.
0–9 answers correct	**Oops!** Time to review what you have learned and try again. Review the practice section on pages 94–113. Then, retake the test on page 114. Now, move on to the section test on page 157.

Mini-Test 3

Page 131

Number Correct

6–8 answers correct	**Great Job!** Move on to the section test on page 157.
4–6 answers correct	**You're almost there!** But you still need a little practice. Review the practice pages 117–130 before moving on to the section test on page 157.
0–3 answers correct	**Oops!** Time to review what you have learned and try again. Review the practice section on pages 117–130. Then, retake the test on page 131. Now, move on to the section test on page 157.

How Am I Doing?

Mini-Test 4 Page 147 **Number Correct**	**7–8** answers correct	**Awesome!** Move on to the section test on page 157.
	5–6 answers correct	**You're almost there!** But you still need a little practice. Review the practice pages 133–146 before moving on to the section test on page 157.
	0–4 answers correct	**Oops!** Time to review what you have learned and try again. Review the practice section on pages 133–146. Then, retake the test on page 147. Now, move on to the section test on page 157.
Mini-Test 5 Page 154 **Number Correct**	**6** answers correct	**Great Job!** Move on to the section test on page 157.
	4–5 answers correct	**You're almost there!** But you still need a little practice. Review the practice pages 149–153 before moving on to the section test on page 157.
	0–3 answers correct	**Oops!** Time to review what you have learned and try again. Review the practice section on pages 149–153. Then, retake the test on page 154. Now, move on to the section test on page 157.

Name _____   Date _____

Final Mathematics Test
For pages 66–154

DIRECTIONS: Choose the best answer.

1. What is the correct numeral for six hundred thirty-eight thousand, nine hundred five?
   - (A) 6,380,950
   - (B) 638,950
   - (C) 638,905
   - (D) 63,895

2. What is 1,240,320 written in expanded form?
   - (F) 100,000 + 20,000 + 4,000 + 300 + 20
   - (G) 1,000,000 + 200,000 + 4,000 + 300 + 2
   - (H) 1,200,000 + 40,000 + 300 + 20
   - (J) 1,000,000 + 200,000 + 40,000 + 300 + 20

3. Which of the following shows 83.586 rounded to the nearest hundredth?
   - (A) 83.00
   - (B) 83.59
   - (C) 83.58
   - (D) 83.50

4. Which of the following are the prime factors for 30?
   - (F) 10 × 3
   - (G) 15 × 2
   - (H) 5 × 6
   - (J) 3 × 5 × 2

5. $13^2 =$ _____
   - (A) 144
   - (B) 256
   - (C) 169
   - (D) 225

6. What is the least common multiple of $\frac{1}{2}$, $\frac{4}{5}$, and $\frac{2}{3}$?
   - (F) 60
   - (G) 15
   - (H) 30
   - (J) 10

7. 435 × 716 = _____
   - (A) 311,460
   - (B) 31,460
   - (C) 2,114,600
   - (D) 214,600

8. 4,550 ÷ 90 = _____
   - (F) 50 R5
   - (G) 45 R50
   - (H) 50 R50
   - (J) 50 R55

9. $\frac{5}{6} + \frac{1}{12} =$ _____
   - (A) $\frac{6}{12}$
   - (B) $1\frac{1}{12}$
   - (C) $\frac{1}{2}$
   - (D) $\frac{11}{12}$

10. $1\frac{1}{12} \times \frac{3}{8} =$ _____
    - (F) $\frac{31}{32}$
    - (G) $\frac{1}{4}$
    - (H) $\frac{3}{32}$
    - (J) $\frac{13}{32}$

11. $\frac{8}{9} \div \frac{1}{4} =$ _____
    - (A) $5\frac{1}{3}$
    - (B) $\frac{1}{36}$
    - (C) $3\frac{5}{9}$
    - (D) $\frac{2}{9}$

GO

Name _____ Date _____

12. What is 0.015 written as a fraction?

    (F) $\frac{15}{100}$ (H) $\frac{15}{1000}$

    (G) $1\frac{5}{10}$ (J) $\frac{15}{10}$

13. Find 854.2 × 56.78.
    (A) 4,850.1476
    (B) 48,501.476
    (C) 485,014.76
    (D) 485.01476

14. A sales tax of 5% is charged on all purchases. What is the sales tax on a purchase of $78?
    (F) $390.00
    (G) $39.00
    (H) $3.90
    (J) $0.39

15. Which group of numbers is ordered from least to greatest?
    (A) −18.29, −12.89, −98.21, −29.81
    (B) −12.47, −12.74, −41.27, −72.14
    (C) −68.24, −86.42, −64.28, −48.26
    (D) −59.73, −57.93, −53.79, −39.75

16. A hiker started out with 48 ounces of water. She drank 9 ounces of water after hiking 5 miles and 16 more ounces when she reached mile marker 8. How many ounces of water did she have left?
    (F) 48 − (9 + 16) = ■
    (G) 48 + (9 − 16) = ■
    (H) (16 − 9) + 48 = ■
    (J) 48 + 9 + 16 = ■

17. A sock drawer has 5 brown pairs of socks, 3 red pairs of socks, and 6 blue pairs of socks. Which of the following does not show the ratio of red to blue?

    (A) $\frac{3}{6}$ (C) $\frac{1}{3}$

    (B) 3:6   (D) 3 to 6

18. $\frac{7}{49} = \frac{12}{n}$
    (F) 54
    (G) 144
    (H) 7
    (J) 84

19. Two triangles are similar. On one triangle, the sides are 4, 5, and 6 units long. The second triangle has sides 8, 10, and x. Use proportions to find x.
    (A) 14
    (B) 6
    (C) 12
    (D) 10

20. 6 L = _____
    (F) 60 mL
    (G) 600 mL
    (H) 6,000 mL
    (J) 60,000 mL

21. 75,000 g = _____
    (A) 7.5 kg
    (B) 75 kg
    (C) 750 kg
    (D) 7,500 kg

22. 1 mile = _____ kilometers
    (F) 2.2
    (G) 2.0
    (H) 1.6
    (J) 1.75

23. Leisha met her friends at the mall at 3:28 P.M. They shopped until 6:00 P.M. How long were they at the mall?
    (A) 3 hours, 2 minutes
    (B) 2 hours, 2 minutes
    (C) 2 hours, 32 minutes
    (D) 3 hours, 32 minutes

GO

Name _____ Date _____

24. Find the area of the triangle.
   F) 8.5 yd.²
   G) 3 yd.²
   H) 2.7 yd.²
   J) 6 yd.²

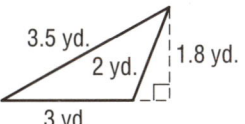

25. Find the area of the parallelogram.
   A) 5.1 m²
   B) 6.46 m²
   C) 2.55 m²
   D) 6.8 m²

DIRECTIONS: Choose the best answer. Use π = 3.14.

26. The area of a circle with a radius of 15 can be written as _____ .
   F) π × 15²
   G) π × 2 × 15
   H) π × 2² × 15
   J) π × 15

27. The area of a circle with a diameter of 4 can be written as _____ .
   A) π × 4
   B) π × 2 × 4
   C) π × ($\frac{1}{2}$ × 4)²
   D) π × 4²

28. What is the area of a circle with a radius of 2?
   F) 50.24
   G) 6.28
   H) 12.56
   J) 25.12

29. What is the circumference of a circle with a diameter of 4?
   A) 50.24
   B) 6.28
   C) 12.56
   D) 25.12

DIRECTIONS: Write the measurement of the missing angle.

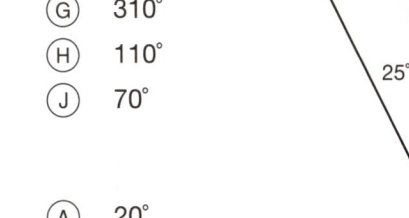

30.
   F) 20°
   G) 310°
   H) 110°
   J) 70°

31.
   A) 20°
   B) 100°
   C) 200°
   D) 160°

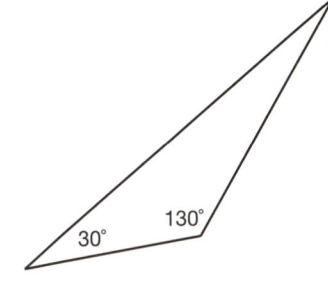

DIRECTIONS: Choose the best answer.

32. An angle that measures 32° is _____ .
   F) acute
   G) obtuse
   H) right
   J) straight

GO

159

Name _____ Date _____

33. A polygon with seven sides is called a(n) _____.

- Ⓐ pentagon
- Ⓑ hexagon
- Ⓒ octagon
- Ⓓ heptagon

34. Which of the following figures is a trapezoid?

- Ⓕ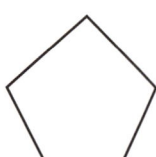
- Ⓖ
- Ⓗ
- Ⓙ

35. Which of the following is *not* a prism?

- Ⓐ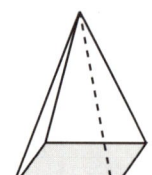
- Ⓑ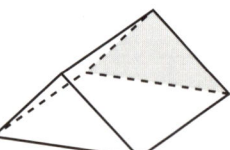
- Ⓒ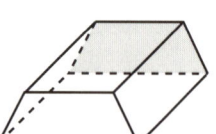
- Ⓓ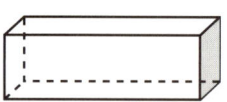

36. A shoe box is 6 inches wide, 11 inches long, and 5 inches high. Find the volume of the box.

- Ⓕ 330 cubic inches
- Ⓖ 22 cubic inches
- Ⓗ 660 cubic inches
- Ⓙ 33 cubic inches

37. This table shows the total number of ice pops contained in different numbers of boxes.

Number of Boxes	Number of Ice Pops
2	24
3	36
4	48
5	60

If the pattern continues, which number sentence shows how you could calculate the number of ice pops in 11 boxes?

- Ⓐ 60 ÷ 11 = ■
- Ⓑ 11 × 12 = ■
- Ⓒ 5 × 11 = ■
- Ⓓ 12 + 60 = ■

38. Which of these are the coordinates of the triangle?

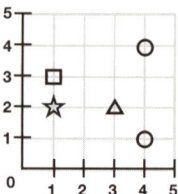

- Ⓕ (1, 2)
- Ⓖ (3, 2)
- Ⓗ (1, 3)
- Ⓙ (4, 4)

39. Which of the following open sentences has the same solution set as 4a + 3 = 27?
    - (A) 3 + a = 15
    - (B) 27 − a = 20
    - (C) 6 × a = 36
    - (D) 60 ÷ a = 12

40. Choose the symbol that would make the following number sentence true.

    5(6 + 7) ☐ 8²

    - (F) <
    - (G) >
    - (H) =
    - (J) None of the above

41. Jacob has a bag with 13 pieces of candy. His father puts some more candy into the bag. He now has 28 pieces. Which equation shows how many pieces his father gave him?
    - (A) 28 ÷ 13 = ■
    - (B) 13 + ■ = 28
    - (C) 28 × 13 = ■
    - (D) 13 − ■ = 28

42. What is the value of y if (8 × y) + 15 = 87?
    - (F) 7
    - (G) 8
    - (H) 9
    - (J) 10

43. The Medina Valley daily newspaper costs $0.35 each day, except for the Sunday edition, which costs $1.25. When Bucky's family went on vacation for 2 weeks, they canceled their subscription for the time they were gone. Which expression can be used to determine how much money they saved by canceling their subscription during their vacation?
    - (A) 7 × (1.25 + 0.35)
    - (B) (2 × 1.35) + (2 × 0.35)
    - (C) (2 × 7) × (1.25 + 0.35)
    - (D) (2 × 6 × 0.35) + (2 × 1.25)

DIRECTIONS: The graph below shows the average number of rainy days per month in Sun City, Florida. Use the graph to answer questions 44–46.

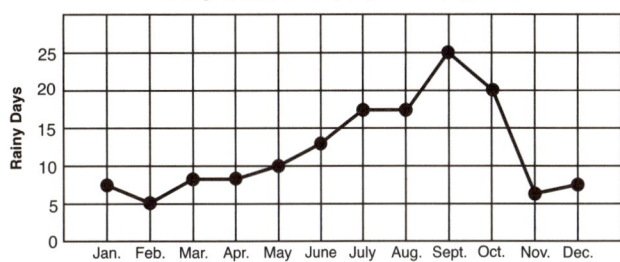

44. Which two-month period shows the greatest change in the number of rainy days?
    - (F) May and June
    - (G) June and July
    - (H) October and November
    - (J) August and September

45. How many inches of rain fell during the rainiest month?
    - (A) 20 inches
    - (B) 25 inches
    - (C) about 18 inches
    - (D) None of the above

46. Based on this graph, which two months should have been the best for tourists?
    - (F) January and February
    - (G) February and November
    - (H) March and April
    - (J) April and December

47. Find the mode for 85, 105, 135, 85, and 65.
    - (A) 70
    - (B) 85
    - (C) 86
    - (D) 95

GO

161

48. Find the median for 85, 105, 135, 85, and 65.
    - (F) 70
    - (G) 85
    - (H) 86
    - (J) 95

49. Find the mean for 85, 105, 135, 85, 65, 80, and 84.
    - (A) 70
    - (B) 85
    - (C) 86
    - (D) 91.3

50. The convenience store has a choice of chocolate, vanilla, and strawberry frozen yogurt in either a sugar cone or a waffle cone. How many choices are there?
    - (F) 9
    - (G) 6
    - (H) 3
    - (J) 5

51. For the previous exercise what is the probability that you will choose a chocolate frozen yogurt on a waffle cone?
    - (A) $\frac{1}{3}$
    - (B) $\frac{1}{5}$
    - (C) $\frac{1}{6}$
    - (D) $\frac{1}{9}$

52. A jar contains 3 red, 5 green, 2 blue, and 6 yellow marbles. A marble is chosen at random from the jar. After replacing it, a second marble is chosen. The probability of getting a green and then a yellow marble is an example of _____ .
    - (F) independent events
    - (G) dependent events

53. Hector's neighborhood is having a rummage sale. The expenses are $10 for flyers, $35 for advertising, and $50 for table rentals. They made a total of $525. How much profit did they make?
    - (A) $620
    - (B) $430
    - (C) $525
    - (D) $95

54. In exercise 24, there were 5 families taking part in the rummage sale. How much does each family get?
    - (F) $105
    - (G) $124
    - (H) $19
    - (J) $86

55. Fifty percent of the people questioned in a sales survey indicated a preference for Brand X. There were 7,520 people questioned. How many of the people questioned preferred Brand X?
    - (A) 3,760
    - (B) 7,520
    - (C) 50
    - (D) 3,500

56. During the sale, Mr. Hansen purchased a coat for 60% off the regular price. The coat normally sold for $220. How much money did he save by buying the coat on sale?
    - (F) $60
    - (G) $220
    - (H) $132
    - (J) $88

STOP

Name _____   Date _____

Final Mathematics Test
Answer Sheet

1. Ⓐ Ⓑ Ⓒ Ⓓ
2. Ⓕ Ⓖ Ⓗ Ⓙ
3. Ⓐ Ⓑ Ⓒ Ⓓ
4. Ⓕ Ⓖ Ⓗ Ⓙ
5. Ⓐ Ⓑ Ⓒ Ⓓ
6. Ⓕ Ⓖ Ⓗ Ⓙ
7. Ⓐ Ⓑ Ⓒ Ⓓ
8. Ⓕ Ⓖ Ⓗ Ⓙ
9. Ⓐ Ⓑ Ⓒ Ⓓ
10. Ⓕ Ⓖ Ⓗ Ⓙ

11. Ⓐ Ⓑ Ⓒ Ⓓ
12. Ⓕ Ⓖ Ⓗ Ⓙ
13. Ⓐ Ⓑ Ⓒ Ⓓ
14. Ⓕ Ⓖ Ⓗ Ⓙ
15. Ⓐ Ⓑ Ⓒ Ⓓ
16. Ⓕ Ⓖ Ⓗ Ⓙ
17. Ⓐ Ⓑ Ⓒ Ⓓ
18. Ⓕ Ⓖ Ⓗ Ⓙ
19. Ⓐ Ⓑ Ⓒ Ⓓ
20. Ⓕ Ⓖ Ⓗ Ⓙ

21. Ⓐ Ⓑ Ⓒ Ⓓ
22. Ⓕ Ⓖ Ⓗ Ⓙ
23. Ⓐ Ⓑ Ⓒ Ⓓ
24. Ⓕ Ⓖ Ⓗ Ⓙ
25. Ⓐ Ⓑ Ⓒ Ⓓ
26. Ⓕ Ⓖ Ⓗ Ⓙ
27. Ⓐ Ⓑ Ⓒ Ⓓ
28. Ⓕ Ⓖ Ⓗ Ⓙ
29. Ⓐ Ⓑ Ⓒ Ⓓ
30. Ⓕ Ⓖ Ⓗ Ⓙ

31. Ⓐ Ⓑ Ⓒ Ⓓ
32. Ⓕ Ⓖ Ⓗ Ⓙ
33. Ⓐ Ⓑ Ⓒ Ⓓ
34. Ⓕ Ⓖ Ⓗ Ⓙ
35. Ⓐ Ⓑ Ⓒ Ⓓ
36. Ⓕ Ⓖ Ⓗ Ⓙ
37. Ⓐ Ⓑ Ⓒ Ⓓ
38. Ⓕ Ⓖ Ⓗ Ⓙ
39. Ⓐ Ⓑ Ⓒ Ⓓ
40. Ⓕ Ⓖ Ⓗ Ⓙ

41. Ⓐ Ⓑ Ⓒ Ⓓ
42. Ⓕ Ⓖ Ⓗ Ⓙ
43. Ⓐ Ⓑ Ⓒ Ⓓ
44. Ⓕ Ⓖ Ⓗ Ⓙ
45. Ⓐ Ⓑ Ⓒ Ⓓ
46. Ⓕ Ⓖ Ⓗ Ⓙ
47. Ⓐ Ⓑ Ⓒ Ⓓ
48. Ⓕ Ⓖ Ⓗ Ⓙ
49. Ⓐ Ⓑ Ⓒ Ⓓ
50. Ⓕ Ⓖ Ⓗ Ⓙ

51. Ⓐ Ⓑ Ⓒ Ⓓ
52. Ⓕ Ⓖ
53. Ⓐ Ⓑ Ⓒ Ⓓ
54. Ⓕ Ⓖ Ⓗ Ⓙ
55. Ⓐ Ⓑ Ⓒ Ⓓ
56. Ⓕ Ⓖ Ⓗ Ⓙ

Answer Key

Page 8
1. play
2. poem
3. fable
4. B
5. H
6. A
7. J
8. B
9. J

Pages 9–10
1. Northern
2. 70; 5,000; 7,800
3. California; two; redwoods; giant sequoias
4. Students should mention reliable resources, such as encyclopedias, educational books and Web sites, and the U.S. Park Service.
5. C
6. Students' summaries should reflect the information in the passage.

Pages 11–12
1. extreme temperatures; little or no vegetation; not much animal life
2. People have adapted their clothing, shelters, and lifestyles to the regions. In Antarctica, people live in research bases. In the Sahara, people live in tents and irrigate their crops.
3. Answers will vary, but students should support their choice with pertinent facts from the article.

Page 13
1. B
2. F
3. D
4. J

Pages 14–15
1. C
2. Answers will vary. The author is likely to disagree with the headline since the article supports the World Series.
3. H
4. most exciting and important sporting event; one of the most popular events each year for sports fans
5. Answers will vary. Students should clearly describe their point of view regarding the World Series.

Pages 16–17
1. expenditures—what you spend your money on; debit—items you subtract from your income; credit—items you add to your income; cash flow—relationship between debits and credits; the amount you spend
2. Step 1—Look at your expenditures. Step 2—Determine debits and credits. Step 3—Determine cash flow and savings.
3. Answers will vary.
4. Answers will vary.

Page 18
Students should identify two reading goals and record their reading for the year.

Page 19 Mini-Test 1
1. D
2. J
3. B
4. G

Page 21
are, is, fly, are, catch, tie, take, dive, keep, are, perch, have
1. are
2. are
3. like
4. are
5. are
6. are
7. is
8. are

Pages 22–23
1. D
2. G
3. C
Webs will vary.

Page 24
1. Mark Twain said, "Work consists of whatever a body is obliged to do. . . . Play consists of whatever a body is not obliged to do."
2. "April prepares her green traffic light and the world thinks *Go*," said Christopher Morley.
3. "That's one small step for a man," said Neil Armstrong, "and one giant leap for mankind."
4. "Injustice anywhere is a threat to justice everywhere," said Martin Luther King, Jr.
5. "Training is everything," said Mark Twain. "The peach was once a bitter almond; cauliflower is nothing but cabbage with a college education."
6. Anne Frank said, "Whoever is happy will make others happy too."
7. "Strength through joy," said Robert Ley.
8. Abraham Lincoln said, "Stand with anybody that stands right. Stand with him while he is right and part with him when he goes wrong."

Page 25
1. car, and
2. ahead; I
3. up, and
4. me; I
5. flying, but
6. Marcy, but
7. stop, or
8. splash; all
9. world, and
10. splash, but
11. Sincerely,
12. Dear Sir:
13. Dear (friend's name, or other greeting),
14. Dear Ms. Sorenson:
15. Dear Julie,
16. Hi, (or any other informal greeting)

Page 26
1. At the grocery store, we need to buy the following: chicken, lettuce, and salad dressing.
2. Matthew likes pepperoni, onion, and green pepper on his pizza.
3. There are five people in our family: Mom, Dad, Jarad, Scott, and me.
4. We need people to play these parts: the detective, the detective's assistant, and the old man.
5. C
6. C
7. Tiffany likes these games: soccer, baseball, and volleyball.
8. C
9. I want to visit these countries: Mexico, Spain, and France.

Pages 27–28
1. B
2. J
3. C
4. G
5. C
6. H
7. A
8. G
9. A
10. H
11. A
12. F
13. C
14. G
15. A
16. H

Page 29
1. present
2. past
3. present
4. present
5. past
6. present
7. present
8. present
9. future
10. future

Pages 30–31
1. B
2. F
3. C
4. G
5. C
6. F
7. C
8. F
9. D
10. H
11. B
12. F
13. B
14. H
15. A
16. J
17. C
18. G

Page 32
1. buy
2. cents
3. due
4. it's
5. there
6. here
7. they're
8. read
9. sent
10. its
11. their
12. threw
13. led
14. where
15. your
16. They're
17. it's
18. you're

Page 33
1. D
2. G
3. A

Pages 34–35
1. A
2. H
3. C
4. H
5. D
6. G
7. D
8. H
9. B

Pages 36–37
1. A
2. H
3. C
4. G
5. B
6. F
7. B
8. H

Page 38
1. B
2. F
3. D
4. J
5. C
6. G
7. A
8. J

Pages 39–40
Mini-Test 2
1. D
2. G
3. A
4. G
5. D
6. G
7. B
8. H
9. D
10. G
11. C
12. G
13. A
14. H
15. D

Page 42
1–4. Students should choose four books with similar themes.
5. Students should identify the similar theme for the four books.
6. Students should mention traits unique to each type of book.
7. Students should mention traits the books have in common.
8. Be sure students offer some support for their opinions.

Pages 43–44
1. metaphor, simile, simile, simile
2. Sollie is not a very good swimmer.
3. B
4. Answers will vary.
5. Sollie would have been better at waterskiing.

Page 45
1. D
2. H
3. A
4. G

Pages 46–47
1. Robin is polite.
   A. She says "thank you."
   B. She brings a hostess gift.
2. Sheila is greedy.
   A. She grabs the candy.
   B. She asks for milk.
3. Tamiko is fearful.
   A. She wants to call her parents.
   B. She brought a flashlight and a teddy bear.
4. Paula is rude.
   A. She uses the phone without first asking for permission.
   B. She asks if her boyfriend can come over.
5. Ted is mischievous.
   A. He is wearing a monster mask.
   B. He plans to scare the girls.

Pages 48–49
1. summer; camp
2. see baby possum/by beech tree/second day; sing songs/in dining hall/every noon; discover blue racer/in field/fifth day; sketch plant specimens/in state forest/rainy day; hear scary stories/in cabin/bedtime; observe raccoons/in woods/one night
3. Students should use the information from the matching activity and add descriptive details to their summaries.

Page 50
1. C
2. J
3. C
4. G

Page 51
1. Rhyme scheme of the poem is a, b, a, b, c, c.
   a—shore, more
   b—see, free
   c—above, love
2. Answers will vary.

Pages 52–53
Theo
  Personality traits—hardworking, disciplined, friendly
  How he feels before the race—very nervous
  What he does during the race—quickly gets into the lead
  What he probably does to finish the race—stays focused to win the race and realize his dream (Answers will vary.)
Carl
  Personality traits—friendly, determined
  How he feels before the race—calm, sure of himself
  What he does during the race—catches up to Theo, who was in the lead
  What he probably does to finish the race—runs hard to try to beat Theo

Page 54
1. B
2. H
3. B
4. G

Page 55
1. Reasons Lee Might Win—campaigned for weeks; prepared speech; has been working hard
   Reasons Kim Might Win—has lots of friends; had a big pool party; wants class to go on lots of field trips
2. Answers will vary. Students should explain why they think Lee or Kim will win the race.

Pages 56–57 Mini-Test 3
1. B
2. H
3. A
4. J
5. B
6. F
7. A
8. H
9. D

Pages 59–62 Final Language Arts Test
1. A
2. H
3. B
4. F
5. C
6. G
7. C
8. H
9. C
10. G
11. C
12. F
13. B
14. G
15. A
16. F
17. C
18. H
19. A

20. H
21. B
22. J
23. A
24. G
25. D

Page 66
1. 562,174
2. 200,518,736
3. 65,270,948,301
4. b
5. a
6. c
7. f
8. d
9. e
10. 711.009, 711.9, 711.95, 712.001, 712.01, 712.09, 712.10

Page 67
1. 102,375.34
2. 25,043.2
3. 782,460.0002
4. 200,104,031.00004
5. 9,650,300
6. 1,000,000 + 200,000 + 300 + 40 + 1
7. 10,000 + 600 + 50 + $\frac{3}{1,000}$
8. 200,000 + 30,000 + 8,000 + 200 + $\frac{5}{100}$
9. 500 + 60 + 3 + $\frac{2}{1,000}$ + $\frac{1}{100,000}$
10. 4,000,000 + 70,000 + 4
11. twenty-three million, forty-two thousand, three hundred sixty-eight
12. four hundred eighteen million, seven hundred twenty-three thousand, six
13. two thousand, seventy-eight and three hundredths
14. thirty thousand twelve and five ten thousandths

Page 68
1. 10
2. 100
3. 1,000
4. 10,000
5. 100,000
6. 1,000,000
7. The power represents the number of zeros.
8. 2,456.9
9. 590
10. 615,892
11. 23.4
12. 68,000
13. 5,349,800
14. 7,640
15. 1,839,426
16. 73,215

Page 69
1. A
2. G
3. D
4. H
5. C
6. F
7. D
8. G

Page 70
1. No. Anita will have approximately $102, which will not be enough money for the CD player. ($8 × 14 hours = $112; $112 − $10 = $102)
2. They will need 3 pizzas, which will cost each person approximately $2. (3 pizzas × $17 = $51; $50 ÷ 25 people = $2 per person.)
3. The floor will cost approximately $260. (13 ft. × 10 ft. = 130 sq. ft.; 130 × $2 = $260)
4. The larger system will cost approximately $32,000 more than the basic system. (38,000 − 6,000 = 32,000)
5. Jorgé will have enough money. (36 + (12 × 4) + (2 × 22) = 128, which is less than $150.)

Page 71
1. Incorrect. Estimate: 700 × 30 = 21,000 Exact: 21,315
2. Correct.
3. Incorrect. Estimate: 80,000 ÷ 40 = 2,000 Exact: 2,183 R7
4. Incorrect. Estimate: 2,000 × 600 = 1,200,000 Exact: 1,496,060
5. Incorrect. Estimate: 1,300,000 + 100,000 = 1,400,000 Exact: 1,373,067
6. Correct.
7. Incorrect. Estimate: 500 × 700 = 350,000 Exact: 323,532
8. Incorrect. Estimate: 400 + 8,000 = 8,400 Exact: 8,320

Page 72
1. 9; 18
2. 15, 3; 45
3. 3; 3; 18
4. 2, 2; 4, 5
5. 5; 4; 40
6. 15, 2; 30
7. 3, 3, 3, 3, 3, 3; 9; 729
8. 2, 2, 9, 4, 4; 36; 144

Page 73
1. B
2. J
3. B
4. F
5. C
6. G
7. C
8. G
9. D
10. H
11. C
12. J

Page 74
1. A
2. J
3. B
4. J
5. B

Page 75
1. C
2. G
3. B
4. J
5. C
6. F
7. A
8. H
9. C
10. J

Page 76
1. B
2. F
3. B
4. H
5. D
6. G
7. C
8. J
9. C
10. G

Page 77

Table 1
- Row 1: $\frac{3}{10}$, $\frac{1}{4}$, $\frac{1}{3}$, $\frac{1}{12}$, $\frac{1}{16}$
- Row 2: $\frac{9}{40}$, $\frac{3}{16}$, $\frac{1}{4}$, $\frac{1}{16}$, $\frac{3}{64}$
- Row 3: $\frac{12}{35}$, $\frac{2}{7}$, $\frac{8}{21}$, $\frac{2}{21}$, $\frac{1}{14}$
- Row 4: $\frac{3}{8}$, $\frac{5}{16}$, $\frac{5}{12}$, $\frac{5}{48}$, $\frac{5}{64}$
- Row 5: $\frac{3}{50}$, $\frac{1}{20}$, $\frac{1}{15}$, $\frac{1}{60}$, $\frac{1}{80}$

Table 2
- Row 1: $\frac{1}{8}$, $\frac{3}{16}$, $\frac{1}{24}$, $\frac{3}{32}$, $\frac{1}{12}$
- Row 2: $\frac{1}{16}$, $\frac{3}{32}$, $\frac{1}{48}$, $\frac{3}{64}$, $\frac{1}{24}$
- Row 3: $\frac{1}{10}$, $\frac{3}{20}$, $\frac{1}{30}$, $\frac{3}{40}$, $\frac{1}{15}$
- Row 4: $\frac{1}{7}$, $\frac{3}{14}$, $\frac{1}{21}$, $\frac{3}{28}$, $\frac{2}{21}$
- Row 5: $\frac{1}{6}$, $\frac{1}{4}$, $\frac{1}{18}$, $\frac{1}{8}$, $\frac{1}{9}$

1. $8\frac{2}{3}$
2. $7\frac{1}{12}$
3. $23\frac{8}{10}$ or $\frac{4}{5}$
4. $32\frac{1}{2}$
5. $25\frac{17}{32}$
6. $4\frac{1}{2}$
12. $5\frac{1}{10}$
13. 4
14. 3
15. $\frac{6}{77}$

Page 78

1. 2
2. $\frac{1}{12}$
3. 0
4. $\frac{2}{15}$
5. $4\frac{1}{2}$
6. $17\frac{3}{5}$
7. $\frac{1}{4}$
8. $\frac{5}{7}$
9. $4\frac{1}{2}$
10. 1
11. $\frac{29}{64}$

Page 79

1. 0.8
2. 0.375
3. 1.67
4. 0.78
5. 0.39
6. 0.07
7. 0.018
8. 1.32
9. 0.0005
10. 87%
11. 120%
12. 45%
13. 2%
14. 34.2%
15. $\frac{6}{10}$ or $\frac{3}{5}$
16. $\frac{42}{100}$ or $\frac{21}{50}$
17. $\frac{25}{1,000}$ or $\frac{1}{40}$
18. $\frac{85}{100}$ or $\frac{17}{20}$
19. $1\frac{92}{100}$ or $1\frac{23}{25}$

Page 80

1. 0.7
2. 0.78
3. 0.75
4. 0.2
5. 0.67
6. 0.625
7. 0.04
8. 8.103
9. 0.3
10. 0.021
11. 0.6
12. 0.5
13. 5.04
14. 1.8
15. 14.07
16. 0.6
17. 0.31
18. 5.024
19. 7.6
20. 15.6
21. 0.25

Page 81

1. 2.55
2. 512.55
3. 577.575
4. 8.39
5. 0.0948672
6. 8.431
7. 0.3933912
8. 27.37427
9. 7.9656
10. 6.254
11. 5.946
12. 4.613

Page 82
PYRAMIDS OF EGYPT

Page 83

1. $\frac{1}{8}$, 0.25, 0.375, 0.625, $\frac{3}{4}$, $\frac{7}{8}$
2. T
3. P
4. M
5. Q
6. N
7. R
8. S
9. L
10. O

Page 84

1. $1,378.98 − $1,050.00 = $328.98
2. $328.98 − $223.42 = $105.56
3. $105.56 − $40.00 = $65.56
4. $65.56 − $36.30 = $29.26
5. $29.26 + $523.81 = $553.07
6. $553.07 − $178.46 = $374.61
7. $374.61 + $30.00 = $404.61
8. $404.61 − $48.23 = $356.38
9. $356.38 − $298.60 = $57.78
10. $57.78 + $40.00 = $97.78
11. An amount less than $97.78 should be entered in the withdrawal column. Balance will vary.
12. Add $523.81 in the deposit column. Balance will vary.

Page 85

1. A
2. G
3. F
4. D
5. C
6. B
7. E
8. H
9. The letter "I" should be written above the 9 on the number line.

Page 86
1. E
2. G
3. D
4. F
5. C
6. A
7. B
8. The letter "I" should be written above $-1\frac{1}{4}$ on the number line.

Page 87
1. 59
2. −184
3. $\frac{3}{4}$
4. 9
5. −5
6. 32
7. 90
8. 126
9. −34
10. 3

Page 88
1. C
2. J
3. B
4. F
5. D
6. G
7. A

Page 89
1. B
2. H
3. A
4. F
5. C
6. H
7. A
8. J
9. C
10. H

Page 90
1. B
2. H
3. D
4. J

Pages 91–92
Mini-Test 1
1. C
2. J
3. C
4. F
5. C
6. G
7. B
8. F
9. B
10. G
11. A
12. J
13. B
14. J
15. C
16. F
17. B
18. H
19. B
20. G

Page 94
1. 4 inches
2. $2\frac{1}{2}$ inches
3. $3\frac{3}{4}$ inches
4. $2\frac{1}{4}$ inches
5. 3 inches
6. $1\frac{1}{2}$ inches
7. $2\frac{1}{4}$ inches
8. $3\frac{7}{8}$ inches

Page 95
1. 1,600 mL
2. 1.621 hL
3. 890 dL
4. 16,000,000 mL
5. 0.09 hL
6. 168,000 cL
7. 6,000 mL
8. 8 cL
9. 60 cL
10. <
11. >
12. =

Page 96
1. 72,000 dg
2. 11,010 mg
3. 1,601.3 dag
4. 6.2 cg
5. 31,000 g
6. 0.0000013 hg
7. 0.219 kg
8. 0.0121 dg
9. 11,610 dg
10. >
11. =
12. <

Page 97
1. 4.8 km
2. 5.45 kg
3. 5 mi.
4. 3 kg
5. 95.45 kg
6. 16 km
7. 2 mi.
8. 6 mi.
9. 36 kg
10. <
11. >
12. =

Page 98
1. B
2. H
3. D
4. G
5. A
6. G
7. C
8. J
9. A
10. G

Page 99
1. Area = 4 cm^2
   Perimeter = 9.6 cm
2. Area = 3.6 m^2
   Perimeter = 8 m
3. Area = 3.525 in.^{2}
   Perimeter = 8.5 in.
4. Area = 48 ft.^{2}
   Perimeter = 32 ft.
5. Area = 2.7 yd.^{2}
   Perimeter = 8.5 yd.
6. Area = 5.1 dm^2
   Perimeter = 10.6 dm

Page 100
1. 45 cm^2
2. 20 in.^{2}
3. 10.5 ft.^{2}
4. 5.325 m^2
5. 12 yd.^{2}

Page 101
1. C = 25.12 in.
   A = 50.24 in.^{2}
2. C = 314 mm
   A = 7,850 mm^2
3. C = 9.42 in.
   A = 7.065 in.^{2}
4. C = 62.8 ft.
   A = 314 ft.^{2}
5. C = 5.024 cm
   A = 2.0096 cm^2
6. C = 3.14 mm
   A = 0.785 mm^2
7. C = 125.6 mm
   A = 1,256 mm^2
8. C = 47.1 in.
   A = 176.625 in.^{2}
9. C = 13.188 m
   A = 13.8474 m^2

Page 102
1. B
2. F
3. C
4. H
5. D
6. J

Page 103
1. A
2. O
3. O
4. R
5. S
6. A
7. R
8. A
9. S
10. O

Page 104
1. right: 60°
2. obtuse: 110°
3. obtuse: 20°
4. acute: 36°
5. acute: 30°
6. acute 50°
7. right: 50°
8. acute: 71°

Page 105
1. C
2. E
3. A
4. B
5. D

Page 106
1. pentagon
2. decagon
3. triangle
4. pentagon
5. dodecagon
6. hexagon
7. octagon
8. quadrilateral (parallelogram)
9. d
10. f
11. b
12. a
13. c
14. e

Page 107
1. rectangle; 90°
2. parallelogram; 128°
3. square; 90°
4. trapezoid; 54°
5. trapezoid; 120°
6. parallelogram; 120°

Page 108
1. pyramid
2. prism
3. pyramid
4. prism
5. neither
6. pyramid
7. pyramid
8. prism
9. prism

Page 109
1. cylinder
2. sphere
3. cone
4. none of these
5. sphere
6. sphere
7. cylinder
8. cone
9. none of these
10. cone
11. none of these
12. sphere

Page 110
1. congruent
2. congruent
3. congruent
4. similar
5. congruent
6. similar
7. congruent
8. similar
9. congruent

Page 111
1. perpendicular
2. perpendicular
3. perpendicular
4. parallel
5. perpendicular
6. parallel
7. neither
8. perpendicular
9. parallel
10. perpendicular
11. neither
12. neither
13. perpendicular

Page 112
1. 180 in.^{3}
2. 198 mm^3
3. 80 cm^3
4. 216 m^3
5. 20 in.^{3}
6. 18 ft.^{3}
7. 40 cm^3
8. 50 m^3
9. 1,792 ft.^{3}

Page 113
1. 12 inches × 9 inches
2. Drawings will vary, but students should include scales, and drawings should reflect the scales.

Pages 114–115
Mini-Test 2
1. A
2. H
3. A
4. J
5. B
6. H
7. A
8. c
9. d
10. f
11. a
12. b
13. e
14. G
15. B
16. J
17. C

Page 117
1. 2,187; 243
2. 20; 24
3. 63; 147
4. 46; 40
5. 24,801,854; 204,974
6. 69; 161
7. 3,483,648; 24,192
8. 150; 175
9. 58; 72
10. 77; 32
11. 32; 128
12. 11; 19
13. 125; 3,125
14. 288; 96
15. 144; 156

Page 118
1. A
2. H
3. A
4. J
5. B
6. F

Page 119
1. A
2. F
3. D
4. G

Page 120
1. B
2. G
3. C
4. H
5. A
6. H
7. A

Page 121

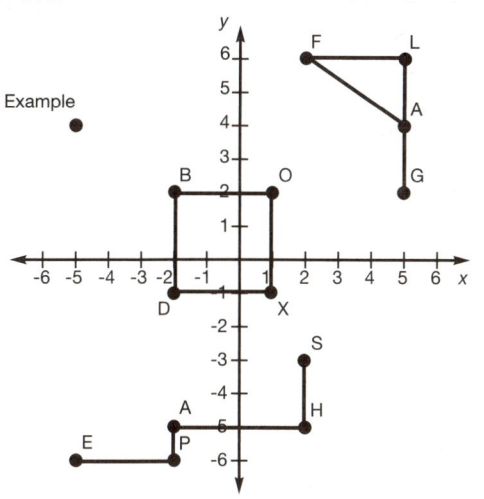

Page 122

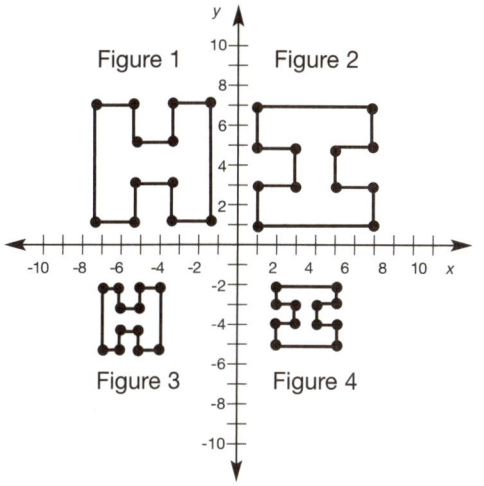

Page 123
1. 21, 23, 25
2. 0, 3, 6, 9, 12, 15
3. 3, 9, 15, 21, 27, 33
4. $y = x + 4$
5. $y = 4x$
6. $y = x - 2$

Page 124
1. C
2. J
3. A
4. H
5. A
6. H
7. A

Page 125
1. D
2. H
3. A
4. G
5. C
6. F
7. A

Page 126
1. 1
2. 2
3. 6
4. 4
5. −4
6. 4
7. 12
8. −7
9. 5
10. 160
11. −9
12. −6

Page 127
1. T
2. F
3. T
4. T
5. F
6. F
7. T
8. F
9. T
10. T
11. F
12. T
13. F
14. T
15. T

Page 128
1. <
2. <
3. >
4. =
5. <
6. >
7. >
8. >
9. =
10. >
11. =
12. >
13. <
14. =
15. <
16. >

Page 129
1. $\frac{1}{3} \times (40 - 10) = n$
2. $n + 97 = 160$ or $160 - 97 = n$
3. $(\$119 - \$99) \times 2 = n$
4. $(12 \times 14) \div 4 = n$
5. $n + 325 = 375$ or $375 - 325 = n$
6. $(9 - 2) \times 12 = n$

Page 130
1. B
2. G
3. B
4. J
5. B
6. G
7. B
8. J

Page 131 Mini-Test 3
1. 859,375; 1,375
2. 1,058,841; 9
3. 240; 360
4. C
5. G
6. B
7. J
8. A

Page 133
1. Last Year: 31 items. This Year: 43 items.
2. 12 items
3. greatest increase: canned goods; decrease: infant clothing
4. There was more variation this year. The difference between the low and high amounts collected per item (the range) was 31. Last year it was 21.

Page 134
1. 10
2. "Number of Students" is a good label to use.
3. 67 people
4.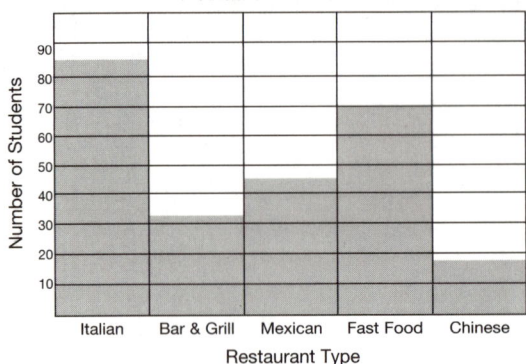

Page 135
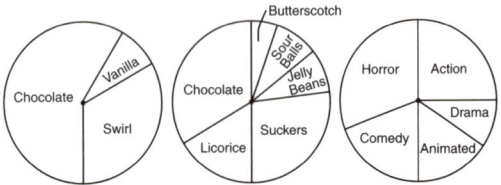

Page 136

Stem	Leaf
3	5, 7, 8
4	1, 3, 4, 5, 5, 7, 8, 9
5	0, 0, 0

The median grade for the math test was 45.

Page 137
1.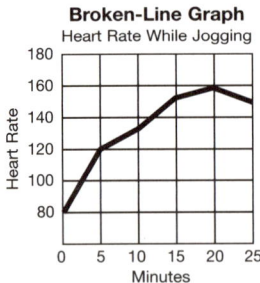
2.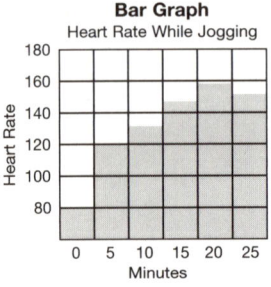

3. 20 minutes
4. between 0 and 5 minutes
5. between 10 and 15 minutes
6. Answers will vary. Students may suggest that the line graph shows the changes in rate more clearly than the bar graph.

Page 138
1.

Member	Popcorn	Pretzels
Amelia	6	12
Bobby	10	12
Carla	14	9
Daniel	15	14
Elizabeth	13	4
Frank	7	15
Gerry	7	5
Hank	12	10
Isabella	1	13
Jim	11	11

2. Daniel; Frank
3. pretzels
4. Daniel; Gerry
5. Students should indicate that using the double bar graph is a more efficient way of showing the data.

Page 139
1. Mean: 44.2
   Median: 45
   Mode: 45
   Range: 50
2. Mean: 48
   Median: 41
   Mode: 35
   Range: 55
3. Mean: 64.1
   Median: 60
   Mode: 85
   Range: 80
4. Mean: 62.7
   Median: 60
   Mode: 60
   Range: 56

5. (Answers will vary.) Store 3 does not have the best variety of prices. Only one brand of shoe was low, creating a large range. However, the average shoe costs $64.1 and half the shoes are over $55.
6. Store 1
7. Store 2 has the best variety of low-priced shoes. The median of $41 tells us that half the shoes cost less than $41.

Page 140
1. B
2. G
3. B
4. F
5. A
6. F
7. Grab 1: $\frac{3}{19}$

   Grab 2: $\frac{3}{18}$ or $\frac{1}{6}$

   Grab 3: $\frac{3}{17}$

   Grab 4: $\frac{3}{16}$

   Grab 5: $\frac{3}{15}$ or $\frac{1}{5}$
8. His chance of getting a licorice jellybean increases with each grab, since there are fewer jellybeans in the bag.
9. $\frac{2}{13}$

Pages 141–142
1. 7
2. 2 and 12
3. 6 and 8
4. $\frac{4}{36}$ or $\frac{1}{9}$
5. $\frac{3}{36} + \frac{4}{36} = \frac{7}{36}$
6. 6 ways; $\frac{6}{36} = \frac{1}{6}$

Sum	Ways to make the sum	# of ways
2		1
3		2
4		3
5		4
6		5
7		6
8		5
9		4
10		3
11		2
12		1
Total		36

Page 143
1. B
2. G
3. D
4. G
5. B
6. J
7. D

Page 144
1. The number of arrangements are 720 (6 × 5 × 4 × 3 × 2 × 1).
2. The number of arrangements are 3,628,800 (10 × 9 × 8 × 7 × 6 × 5 × 4 × 3 × 2 × 1).

Page 145
1. 2 × 2 × 2 × 2 = 16
2. 3 × 6 × 3 = 54
3. 5 × 5 × 3 = 75

Page 146
1. A
2. F
3. B
4. H
5.
- ham — white, wheat, rye
- beef — white, wheat, rye
- turkey — white, wheat, rye
- bologna — white, wheat, rye

6.
- black — leather, fabric
- red — leather, fabric
- tan — leather, fabric

Page 147 Mini-Test 4
1. C
2. H
3. B
4. H
5.

Stem	Leaf
7	0, 4, 5, 6
8	1, 6, 9
9	2, 4, 7

6. A
7. G
8. A

Page 149
1. B
2. F
3. D
4. F
5. C
6. J
7. A
8. G

Pages 150–151
1. A
2. G
3. B
4. G
5. C
6. J
7. D
8. H
9. A
10. F
11. D
12. H

Page 152
1. B
2. J
3. A
4. G
5. A
6. G
7. A
8. H

Page 153
1. C
2. G
3. D
4. J
5. B

Page 154 Mini-Test 5
1. B
2. J
3. A
4. H
5. C
6. G

Pages 157–162 Final Mathematics Test
1. C
2. J
3. B
4. J
5. C
6. H
7. A
8. H
9. D
10. J
11. C
12. H
13. B
14. H
15. D
16. F
17. C
18. J
19. C
20. H
21. B
22. H
23. C
24. H
25. A
26. F
27. C
28. H
29. C
30. H
31. A
32. F
33. D
34. H
35. D
36. F
37. B
38. G
39. C
40. G
41. B
42. H
43. D
44. H
45. B
46. G
47. B
48. G
49. D
50. G
51. C
52. F
53. B
54. J
55. A
56. H

New York State Standards

Language Arts

Standard 1—Language for Information and Understanding
Intermediate

Listening and Reading

1.1 Listening and reading to acquire information and understanding involves collecting data, facts, and ideas; discovering relationships, concepts, and generalizations; and using knowledge from oral, written, and electronic sources.

Students:

- **1.1A** interpret and analyze information from textbooks and nonfiction books for young adults, as well as reference materials, audio and media presentations, oral interviews, graphs, charts, diagrams, and electronic data bases intended for a general audience.
- **1.1B** compare and synthesize information from different sources.
- **1.1C** use a wide variety of strategies for selecting, organizing, and categorizing information.
- **1.1D** distinguish between relevant and irrelevant information and between fact and opinion.
- **1.1E** relate new information to prior knowledge and experience.
- **1.1F** understand and use the text features that make information accessible and usable, such as format, sequence, level of diction, and relevance of details.

What it means:
- produce a summary of the information about a famous person found in a biography, encyclopedia, and textbook.
- use facts and data from news articles and television reports in an oral report on a current event.
- compile a bibliography of sources that are used in a research project.
- take notes that record the main ideas and most significant supporting details of a lecture or speech.

Speaking and Writing

1.2 Speaking and writing to acquire and transmit information requires asking probing and clarifying questions, interpreting information in one's own words, applying information from one context to another, and presenting the information and interpretation clearly, concisely, and comprehensibly.

Students:

- **1.2A** produce oral and written reports on topics related to all school subjects.
- **1.2B** establish an authoritative stance on the subject and provide references to establish the validity and verifiability of the information presented.
- **1.2C** organize information according to an identifiable structure, such as compare/contrast or general to specific.
- **1.2D** develop information with appropriate supporting material, such as facts, details, illustrative examples or anecdotes, and exclude extraneous material.

1.2E use the process of pre-writing, drafting, revising, and proofreading (the "writing process") to produce well constructed informational texts.

1.2F use standard English for formal presentation of information, selecting appropriate grammatical constructions and vocabulary, using a variety of sentence structures, and observing the rules of punctuation, capitalization, and spelling.

What it means:
- write an essay for science class that contains information from interviews, data bases, magazines, and science texts.
- participate in a panel discussion on population trends in the United States in recent years, using graphics, and citing the source of the data.
- use technical terms correctly in subject area reports.
- survey student views on a school issue and report findings to the class.

Standard 2—Language for Literary Response and Expression
Intermediate

Listening and Reading
2.1 Listening and reading for literary response involves comprehending, interpreting, and critiquing imaginative texts in every medium, drawing on personal experiences and knowledge to understand the text, and recognizing the social, historical, and cultural features of the text.

Students:
2.1A read and view texts and performances from a wide range of authors, subjects, and genres.

2.1B understand and identify the distinguishing features of the major genres and use them to aid their interpretation and discussion of literature.

2.1C identify significant literary elements (including metaphor, symbolism, foreshadowing, dialect, rhyme, meter, irony, climax) and use those elements to interpret the work.

2.1D recognize different levels of meaning.

2.1E read aloud with expression, conveying the meaning and mood of a work.

2.1F evaluate literary merit based on an understanding of the genre and the literary elements.

What it means:
- read or recite poems of their own selection to the class, clearly conveying the meaning of the poem and the effect of the rhythm and rhyme patterns.
- produce lists of recommended readings for their peers, grouping the works according to some common elements (e.g., theme, setting, type of characters).
- use references to literature they have read to support their position in class discussion.

Speaking and Writing
2.2 Speaking and writing for literary response involves presenting interpretations, analyses, and reactions to the content and language of a text. Speaking and writing for literary expression involves producing imaginative texts that use language and text structures that are inventive and often multilayered.

Students:
- **2.2A** present responses to and interpretations of literature, making reference to the literary elements found in the text and connections with their personal knowledge and experience.
- **2.2B** produce interpretations of literary works that identify different levels of meaning and comment on their significance and effect.
- **2.2C** write stories, poems, literary essays, and plays that observe the conventions of the genre and contain interesting and effective language and voice.
- **2.2D** use standard English effectively.

What it means:
- take part in class productions of short plays.
- write a sequel to a story continuing the development of the characters, plot, and themes.
- write reviews of literature from different cultural settings and point out similarities and differences in that literature.
- write stories or poems for their peers or younger children.

Standard 3—Language for Critical Analysis and Evaluation
Intermediate

Listening and Reading

3.1 Listening and reading to analyze and evaluate experiences, ideas, information, and issues requires using evaluative criteria from a variety of perspectives and recognizing the difference in evaluations based on different sets of criteria.

Students:
- **3.1A** analyze, interpret, and evaluate information, ideas, organization, and language from academic and nonacademic texts, such as textbooks, public documents, book and movie reviews, and editorials.
- **3.1B** assess the quality of texts and presentations, using criteria related to the genre, the subject area, and purpose (e.g., using the criteria of accuracy, objectivity, comprehensiveness, and understanding of the game to evaluate a sports editorial).
- **3.1C** understand that within any group there are many different points of view depending on the particular interests and values of the individual, and recognize those differences in perspective in texts and presentations (e.g., in considering whether to let a new industry come into a community, some community members might be enthusiastic about the additional jobs that will be created while others are concerned about the air and noise pollution that could result).
- **3.1D** evaluate their own and others' work based on a variety of criteria (e.g., logic, clarity, comprehensiveness, conciseness, originality, conventionality) and recognize the varying effectiveness of different approaches.

What it means:
- compare a magazine article on a historical event with the entries in an encyclopedia and history book to determine the accuracy and comprehensiveness of the article.
- use the criteria of scientific investigation to evaluate the significance of a lab experiment.
- read two conflicting reviews of a popular movie and recognize the different criteria the critics were using to evaluate the film.
- point out examples of propaganda techniques (such as "bandwagon," "plain folks" language, and "sweeping generalities") in public documents and speeches.

Speaking and Writing

3.2 Speaking and writing for critical analysis and evaluation requires presenting opinions and judgments on experiences, ideas, information, and issues clearly, logically, and persuasively with reference to specific criteria on which the opinion or judgment is based.

Students:

3.2A present (in essays, position papers, speeches, and debates) clear analyses of issues, ideas, texts, and experiences, supporting their positions with well developed arguments.

3.2B develop arguments with effective use of details and evidence that reflect a coherent set of criteria (e.g., reporting results of lab experiments to support a hypothesis).

3.2C monitor and adjust their own oral and written presentations according to the standards for a particular genre (e.g., defining key terms used in a formal debate).

3.2D use standard English, precise vocabulary, and presentational strategies effectively to influence an audience.

What it means:
- write a position paper on a current event, clearly indicating their position and the criteria on which it is based.
- present an oral review of a film, supporting their evaluation with reference to particular elements such as character development, plot, pacing, and cinematography.
- participate in a class debate on a social issue following the rules for formal debate.
- produce their own advertising for a product, tailoring the text and visuals to a particular audience.

Standard 4—Language for Social Interaction
Intermediate

Listening and Speaking

4.1 Oral communication in formal and informal settings requires the ability to talk with people of different ages, genders, and cultures, to adapt presentations to different audiences, and to reflect on how talk varies in different situations.

Students:

- **4.1A** listen attentively to others and build on others' ideas in conversations with peers and adults.
- **4.1B** express ideas and concerns clearly and respectfully in conversations and group discussions.
- **4.1C** learn some words and expressions in another language to communicate with a peer or adult who speaks that language.
- **4.1D** use verbal and nonverbal skills to improve communication with others.

What it means:
- act as hosts for open house at school.
- participate in small group discussions in class.
- give morning announcements over the public address system.
- participate in school assemblies and club meetings.

Reading and Writing

4.2 Written communication for social interaction requires using written messages to establish, maintain, and enhance personal relationships with others.

Students:

- **4.2A** write social letters, cards, and electronic messages to friends, relatives, community acquaintances, and other electronic network users.
- **4.2B** use appropriate language and style for the situation and the audience and take into account the ideas and interests expressed by the person receiving the message.
- **4.2C** read and discuss social communications and electronic communications of other writers and use some of the techniques of those writers in their own writing.

What it means:
- write letters to friends who are away.
- send e-mail messages on a computer network.
- send formal invitations for receptions or open houses.

New York State Standards

Mathematics

Standard 1—Analysis, Inquiry, and Design
Intermediate

Mathematical Analysis

1.1 Abstraction and symbolic representation are used to communicate mathematically.

Students:

    1.1A extend mathematical notation and symbolism to include variables and algebraic expressions in order to describe and compare quantities and express mathematical relationships.

1.2 Deductive and inductive reasoning are used to reach mathematical conclusions.

Students:

    1.2A use inductive reasoning to construct, evaluate, and validate conjectures and arguments, recognizing that patterns and relationships can assist in explaining and extending mathematical phenomena.

What it means:
- predict the next triangular number by examining the pattern 1, 3, 6, 10, ■.

1.3 Critical thinking skills are used in the solution of mathematical problems.

Students:

    1.3A apply mathematical knowledge to solve real-world problems and problems that arise from the investigation of mathematical ideas, using representations such as pictures, charts, and tables.

Standard 3—Mathematics
Intermediate

Mathematical Reasoning

3.1 Students use mathematical reasoning to analyze mathematical situations, make conjectures, gather evidence, and construct an argument.

Students:

    3.1A apply a variety of reasoning strategies.
    3.1B make and evaluate conjectures and arguments using appropriate language.
    3.1C make conclusions based on inductive reasoning.
    3.1D justify conclusions involving simple and compound (i.e., and/or) statements.

What it means:
- use trial and error and work backwards to solve a problem.
- identify patterns in a number sequence.
- are asked to find numbers that satisfy two conditions, such as $n > -4$ and $n < 6$.

Number and Numeration

3.2 Students use number sense and numeration to develop an understanding of the multiple uses of numbers in the real world, the use of numbers to communicate mathematically, and the use of numbers in the development of mathematical ideas.

Students:

3.2A understand, represent, and use numbers in a variety of equivalent forms (integer, fraction, decimal, percent, exponential, expanded and scientific notation).

3.2B understand and apply ratios, proportions, and percents through a wide variety of hands-on explorations.

3.2C develop an understanding of number theory (primes, factors, and multiples).

3.2D recognize order relations for decimals, integers, and rational numbers.

What it means:
- use prime factors of a group of denominators to determine the least common denominator.
- select two pairs from a number of ratios and prove that they are in proportion.
- demonstrate the concept that a number can be symbolized by many different numerals as in:

$$\frac{1}{4} = \frac{3}{12} = \frac{25}{100} = 0.25 = 25\%$$

Operations

3.3 Students use mathematical operations and relationships among them to understand mathematics.

Students:

3.3A add, subtract, multiply, and divide fractions, decimals, and integers.

3.3B explore and use the operations dealing with roots and powers.

3.3C use grouping symbols (parentheses) to clarify the intended order of operations.

3.3D apply the associative, commutative, distributive, inverse, and identity properties.

3.3E demonstrate an understanding of operational algorithms (procedures for adding, subtracting, etc.).

3.3F develop appropriate proficiency with facts and algorithms.

3.3G apply concepts of ratio and proportion to solve problems.

What it means:
- create area models to help in understanding fractions, decimals, and percents.
- find the missing number in a proportion in which three of the numbers are known, and letters are used as place holders.
- arrange a set of fractions in order, from the smallest to the largest:
$$\frac{3}{4}, \frac{1}{5}, \frac{2}{3}, \frac{1}{2}, \frac{1}{4}$$
- illustrate the distributive property for multiplication over addition, such as $2(a + 3) = 2a + 6$.

Modeling/Multiple Representation

3.4 Students use mathematical modeling/multiple representation to provide a means of presenting, interpreting, communicating, and connecting mathematical information and relationships.

Students:

- **3.4A** visualize, represent, and transform two- and three-dimensional shapes.
- **3.4B** use maps and scale drawings to represent real objects or places.
- **3.4C** use the coordinate plane to explore geometric ideas.
- **3.4D** represent numerical relationships in one- and two-dimensional graphs.
- **3.4E** use variables to represent relationships.
- **3.4F** use concrete materials and diagrams to describe the operation of real world processes and systems.
- **3.4G** develop and explore models that do and do not rely on chance.
- **3.4H** investigate both two- and three-dimensional transformations.
- **3.4I** use appropriate tools to construct and verify geometric relationships.
- **3.4J** develop procedures for basic geometric constructions.

What it means:
- build a city skyline to demonstrate skill in linear measurements, scale drawing, ratio, fractions, angles, and geometric shapes.
- bisect an angle using a straight edge and compass.
- draw a complex of geometric figures to illustrate that the intersection of a plane and a sphere is a circle or point.

Standard 3—Mathematics
Intermediate

Measurement

3.5 Students use measurement in both metric and English measure to provide a major link between the abstractions of mathematics and the real world in order to describe and compare objects and data.

Students:

- **3.5A** estimate, make, and use measurements in real-world situations.
- **3.5B** select appropriate standard and nonstandard measurement units and tools to measure to a desired degree of accuracy.
- **3.5C** develop measurement skills and informally derive and apply formulas in direct measurement activities.
- **3.5D** use statistical methods and measures of central tendencies to display, describe, and compare data.
- **3.5E** explore and produce graphic representations of data using calculators/computers.
- **3.5F** develop critical judgment for the reasonableness of measurement.

What it means:
- use box plots or stem and leaf graphs to display a set of test scores.
- estimate and measure the surface areas of a set of gift boxes in order to determine how much wrapping paper will be required.
- explain when to use mean, median, or mode for a group of data.

Uncertainty

3.6 Students use ideas of uncertainty to illustrate that mathematics involves more than exactness when dealing with everyday situations.

Students:

- **3.6A** use estimation to check the reasonableness of results obtained by computation, algorithms, or the use of technology.
- **3.6B** use estimation to solve problems for which exact answers are inappropriate.
- **3.6C** estimate the probability of events.
- **3.6D** use simulation techniques to estimate probabilities.
- **3.6E** determine probabilities of independent and mutually exclusive events.

What it means:
- construct spinners to represent random choice of four possible selections.
- perform probability experiments with independent events (e.g., the probability that the head of a coin will turn up, or that a 6 will appear on a die toss).
- estimate the number of students who might choose to eat hot dogs at a picnic.

Patterns/Functions

3.7 Students use patterns and functions to develop mathematical power, appreciate the true beauty of mathematics, and construct generalizations that describe patterns simply and efficiently.

Students:

- **3.7A** recognize, describe, and generalize a wide variety of patterns and functions.
- **3.7B** describe and represent patterns and functional relationships using tables, charts and graphs, algebraic expressions, rules, and verbal descriptions.
- **3.7C** develop methods to solve basic linear and quadratic equations.
- **3.7D** develop an understanding of functions and functional relationships: that a change in one quantity (variable) results in change in another.
- **3.7E** verify results of substituting variables.
- **3.7F** apply the concept of similarity in relevant situations.
- **3.7G** use properties of polygons to classify them.
- **3.7H** explore relationships involving points, lines, angles, and planes.
- **3.7I** develop and apply the Pythagorean principle in the solution of problems.
- **3.7J** explore and develop basic concepts of right triangle trigonometry.
- **3.7K** use patterns and functions to represent and solve problems.

What it means:

- find the height of a building when a 20-foot ladder reaches the top of the building when its base is 12 feet away from the structure.
- investigate number patterns through palindromes (pick a 2-digit number, reverse it and add the two—repeat the process until a palindrome appears).

```
                    42         86
                   +24        +68
        palindrome  66        154
                              +451
                              605
                              +506
        palindrome           1111
```

- solve linear equations, such as $2(x + 3) = x + 5$ by several methods.

NOTES